Family Spaces

Family Spaces

Creative Solutions for Family-Friendly Interiors

Tirzah Ortiz-Wanlass and P. Jonathan Ortiz

photographs by Lars Jagatai Bunch

Gibbs Smith, Publisher
Salt Lake City

Dedication
From our family to yours—T. W. & J. O.

First
Edition
07 06 05 04 03
5 4 3 2 1

Text © 2003 by Tirzah Wanlass
and Jonathan Ortiz
Photographs © 2003 by Lars Jagatai Bunch

Published by
Gibbs Smith, Publisher
P.O. Box 667
Layton, Utah 84041

1-800-748-5439 orders
www.gibbs-smith.com

Book designed by James Reyman Studio
Printed and bound in Hong Kong

Library of Congress Cataloging-in-Publication Data

Wanlass, Tirzah.
Family spaces: creative solutions for family-friendly interiors / Tirzah Wanlass
and Jonathan Ortiz;
photographs by Lars Jagatai Bunch.—1st ed.
p. cm
ISBN 1-58685-277-9
1. Interior design—United States—History —20th century.
I. Ortiz, Jonathan. II. Title.
NK2004. W36 2003
747—dc21   2003007505

Contents

Acknowledgements

Dirk, Lacey Ellen, Shane, Lucas, and Locksley Hannah—Where would I be without you all? You are my daily inspiration, and you teach me to appreciate, laugh at, and embrace life. You are what this book is about.

Thank you, Paris, Maria, Sally, and Christine—Our countless conversations filled with your wisdom, support, and encouragement remind me that true friends are so rare and just how blessed I am to know you.

The fabulous Queen of Country, Mary Emmerling—Thank you for seeing something in me I didn't fully realize and opening my eyes to opportunity, possibility, and creative growth.

Molly English—Thank you for remembering me when you didn't have to. I will always remember you.

My in-laws, Jay and Eloise—You have always been there, no matter what. Thank you for your constant smiles and tender hearts.

My father, Joe. I love you dearly. Thank you for teaching me the meaning of unconditional love.

And Peter (my twin brother who just happens to be ten years younger than I am!)— I am so grateful for our bond—for the laughter, the tears, and our "psychic connection." I am so proud of the passionate, thoughtful (and thought-provoking), giving, and incredibly talented person you are. Thank you for being an awesome brother, a phenomenal uncle, and an even better friend!

—*T.W.*

HOW CAN I EVER ACCURATELY OR COMPLETELY express my absolute gratitude to those special people who have both directly and indirectly contributed to the completion of this project? Words fail me—but I'll try a little something.

Truly I have been blessed with the most tremendous family. Tirzah—Sister, you are my inspiration. You are all that I could possibly hope to be, embodying all that is pure and good in my life. You fuel my dreams for tomorrow and provide me with the stamina for today—thank you, thank you, thank you.

My brother (in-law) Dirk—Thank you for your support (in innumerable ways) and simple guidance. I am truly and forever grateful.

Lacey Ellen (soon to be super-model!)—You are the proof that "fabulous" is not just an adjective.

Shane, future Olympic and/or Professional/Extreme Sports Champion—Your dogged determination and untiring grit consistently motivate me to press on.

Luke and Locksley—The laughter and innocent pleasure that you still find in life is a constant reminder of all that is truly important. Thanks.

My very dearest and unquestioningly best friends Miranda and Michael, Yess and Chels—Where would I be without you guys? You are my pride and my strength. I look to you for sustenance and advice, and point to you as my heroes! I cannot wait to see where life takes you, and I sit content, knowing that it's just a question of time!

My father, Joseph—I sit in awe of your spirit and am utterly amazed at your life. Thank you for teaching me that, ultimately, all things work together for the glory of God.

And of course my "Lovelies" in New Orleans—All I do is for you. Thank you for always being there.

Jay and Eloise Wanlass—Thank you for allowing me to be family and supporting me like one of your own.

I also owe much of the time and energy that this book required to my professors—no, my friends (Dr. Hina Azam, Dr. Michael Barram, Dr. Paul Giurlanda, Dr. Carol Manahan, and Dr. Norrie Palmer)—at St. Mary's College in Moraga—Your encouragement and example are the only reasons I was physically and mentally able to even contemplate such an attempt. You are educators in every sense of the word. From the bottom of my heart, thank you!

And finally, but by no means lastly, thank you to the seven (plus one, my sister's) talented, creative, ingenious, amazing, stylish, warm, beautiful families who allowed my sister and me to invade their homes for days on end! This book is nothing short of a tribute to you and your miraculous abilities.   —*J.O.*

Introduction

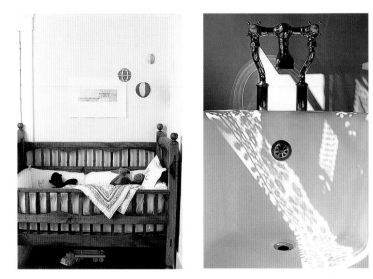

HAVE YOU EVER BEEN STANDING in line at the grocery store and happen to glance at the magazine racks strategically placed around you? You're bored, a little tired, and your eyes lethargically roam across those magazines and their glossy covers. Then one catches your eye. It displays a sumptuously lavish master bedroom complete with gold gilding and four posts with an obscenely oversized bed wrapped in layers of linens that cost more than you could sell your right kidney for. Beside the bed, a massive fireplace glows with the warm hum of a neatly burning pile of wood, and on the floor a plush Persian rug invites you to stretch out.

Your mind starts to wander into delectable dreams of the beautiful lifestyle and you think, "If only I could get onto one of those TV shows where they come and transform my house . . ." You pick up the publication and flip through it until you reach the cover-page article. After multiple images of remarkable rooms and fabulous furnishings, just when you feel your personal creativity store has been replenished with the inspiration to make your home "just like this one, " you read in the article's last paragraph that this is the home of Mr. and Mrs. Hollywood and the wonderful result of Mr. Interior Design and his entourage of design experts for the affordable fee of, oh, just a gazillion dollars! Just then, a bubble-bursting voice intrudes your daydream to inquire if you want "paper or plastic?"

Don't be embarrassed; we've all been there, gazing longingly at the multitude of palatial homes belonging to people we will probably never meet. All just to have that posh Persian rug ripped right out from beneath us by the stifling truths of an all-too-often economically fueled reality. For those of us who live in the real world of finance- and time-concious budgets, with kids or a career or whatever, those magazines and/or decorating books are little more than a frustrating tease.

Well, get out of those books and get into ours. Shameless, huh? But, really, let's face it. When you have a bottomless pocketbook, regardless of your degree of talent or creative inclinations, your home can always be a showplace—it doesn't require creativity or talent to hire a designer. Similarly, in the world of design, the idea of having a family is usually seen as a trade-off for that of a stylish anything, especially home. Kids, pets, other people mean the necessary end of the window for fashionable opportunity, right? No, you need to find realistic sources not just for empty encouragement but for sound advice in attaining your goal. You can have a gorgeous home, a creative home, a stylized home. Don't be persuaded to accept the ordinary because you think anything beyond that is not practical or functional or livable. This book is about just such people, and their tips for practical application to your home, your life. There are no magic solutions, just real families and their real lives. We can't promise the exact duplication of the spaces you'll see here, but we can promise genuine inspiration, hopefully resulting in some real motivation.

Walk with us through the lives and homes of eight, 100-percent real families. They could easily be your next-door neighbors or coworkers. They come from various backgrounds and a wide range of places. Their homes are in big cities and small towns, old and new, large and small. While their styles vary from modern to antique, they are consistently beautiful and absolutely attainable. Through the common use of neutral backdrops, seasonal accents, unique storage solutions, a careful attention to a cost-effective budget, and the realization that true "family rooms" are not static but constantly evolving, they have formulated distinct answers to true decorator challenges, creating their own signature style. They have all found the soothing calm that their homes can—no, should—offer and continue to build on the assumption that the craziness of a modern lifestyle dictates that your home must be your refuge, full of your favorite things and people you love, and the place where you can recharge. We'll tour their homes from the front door to the backyard and enjoy their amazing creations. Let them stimulate within you the sureties that "if they can do it, so can I."

Across the living room, a French youth bed lined in black linen cushions and set below a tone-on-tone painting provides additional seating, ultimately becoming a work of art in itself.

CHAPTER ONE

French Flea Market

THE TESTU FAMILY HOME

OFTEN BEGINNING THEIR mornings just over the hill at the beach or around the corner at the park, Fred, Wendy, and Lolita (two years old) have truly found a little piece of heaven. Whether it be surfing (Fred), ceramics or yoga (Wendy), or contemplative painting (Lolita), the location provides inspiration and opportunity for all of their favorite activities. And while this trio enjoys attending local art and restaurant openings, entertaining friends and family at home has always been a treasured experience. Though their well-worn antiques may look delicate and fragile, don't be fooled: they have proven to be both rugged and toddler-proof. Everything has been varnished to protect both the pieces themselves and little Lolita. And having already lived through a lifetime of their own, the furnishings don't mind another ding or even stain. The creation of their "look" was a pensive procedure. Beginning with a fresh coat of paint, filling the space took some particular planning. But no worries, the family liked the process. "We lived in it empty for a while and enjoyed it." In the end, though, it

The Testu Family Portrait (from left): Lolita, Wendy, and Fred.

◁ A salvaged three-legged stool provides a perfect platform for this beautifully kept antique accordion.

▷ Placing a pineapple head inside a vase creates a holistic and intriguing display.

▽ Atop a rolling cart, now used as a side table, a rectangular tray filled with various eggs is accompanied by vibrant green blooms in a rusted urn.

was definitely worth it! With a collection of randomly placed artifacts and creative attention to detail, the Testu home has become a work of art all their own.

The Testu home lies among the countless common rows of one of San Francisco's closely packed districts of miniature Victorians. Over a steep hill and along its winding road, the quiet neighborhood and its inconspicuous dwellings rest as they have for nearly a century. And while each looks intensely similar to the one right next to it, Wendy and Fred's home hides something vaguely foreign and altogether unique from its neighbors. Their home, with its delightful design, has an extraordinary look that we've dubbed *French Flea Market*.

The Testu team began ten years ago while both were working in the clothing design industry. With Wendy's devotion to sculpting and Fred's love of photography, the two shared an immediate passion for artistic creativity. After their marriage in France, Fred's birthplace, the newlyweds moved into the heart of downtown San Francisco. The city's natural beauty and inspirational architecture motivated an enthusiasm for the collection of recycled furnishings, "French junk" as Wendy calls it, much of which resulted from their visits back to Fred's home.

WITH FLAGRANT DISREGARD for original intent, *French Flea Market* seeks to reclaim rescued treasures, giving them new place and purpose. It's the creative and functional reuse of tossed away and forgotten objects. A clean, open, and bright space is ironically composed of old, weathered, reincarnated rubbish. Though formerly situated in estates and grand chateaux, like a breath of fresh air, they have been reestablished in simple, more comfortable places.

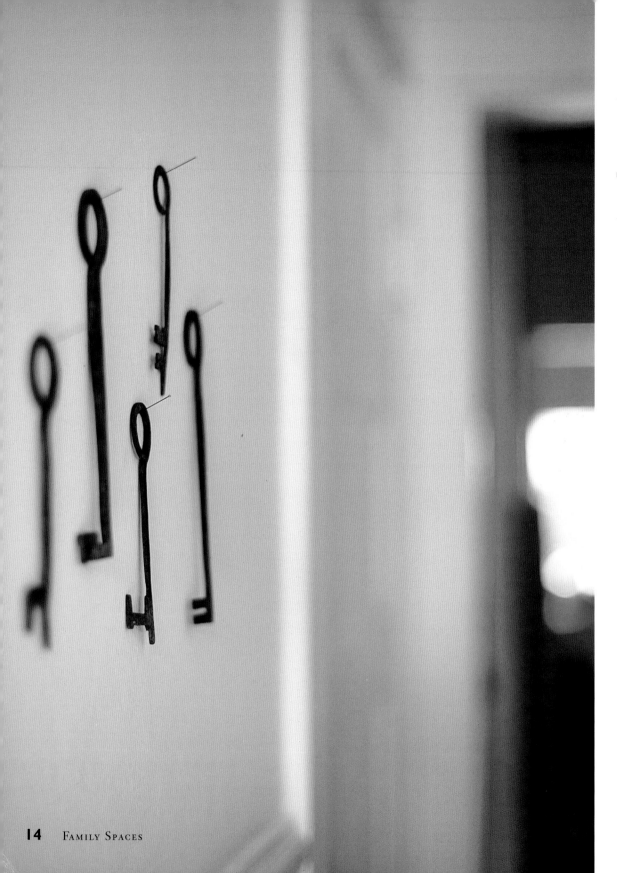

◁ **A gathering of skeleton keys makes a simple statement when grouped as a collection.**

▷ **Fred's passion for photography has provided him with many incredible pictures, but the collage in the hallway is a unique alternative to the traditional family portrait, commemorating their most special moments.**

WHEN ENTERING FRED AND WENDY'S home, the initial impression is a bit deceiving. The long, narrow entry hall appears mundane; however, upon closer examination, we encounter tidbits of the Testu talent. Created by Fred, a basic grouping of ancient skeleton keys contrasts the intricate photographic collage on opposing walls. It is an artfully sophisticated alternative to the family portrait. They are held together with simple straight pins, and the result is an easily attainable, dramatic effect. As with a box of chocolates, following our first taste we couldn't wait to see what was next.

THE TESTU LIVING ROOM is like a dream. The light pouring in through the windows, the stark white walls, and the detailed furnishings combine to create a mystical spot. The room's furnishings are mismatched, the grouping unexpected: two iron youth beds, well worn from years of use, now provide occasional seating, while the salvaged garden Madonna stands as a conversation piece for a leather side chair and its weathered-iron mate. Remnants of a bistro table now topped with glass cozy up "sofa"side and serve as flower stand, console, bookshelf, or whatever. For Wendy the challenge in flower arranging is being able to use whatever is at hand or in the yard. In this room a cluster of three vintage apothecary jars have been recycled to hold monochromatic arrangements gathered from the outside. The light that fills the room filters easily through the clever window treatments—cheesecloth right out of the box, slung over a basic iron rod. Except for a few hanging sculptures, the walls are stunningly bare.

▲ **A row of lidded canisters is a clever and stylish way to store souvenirs from summer vacation.**

◄ **A powerful and inspirational effect is created by the room's very minimal decor.** *(inset)* **Wendy and Lolita relax and enjoy quality time on the comfy living room "sofa."**

▶ **An assortment of three antique apothecary jars holds the stocks of monochromatic flower arrangements.**

REFLECTING THE TRANQUILITY of this space, the dining room, too, is bare yet powerful. The dark wood French farm table is lined with white metal patio chairs. Wendy has sculpted an enchanting display in place of a customary centerpiece. A strong but quiet backdrop, a large "built-in" shelters other flea market finds accompanied by more of Wendy's original pieces. She adds fresh fruits with vivid color for a punch of life (and a savory treat for Lolita). Finishing the space, a salvaged three-legged stool nestled in the corner bears a beautiful antique accordion.

▲ A Testu original, Wendy's art fills the house and serves here as the table's centerpiece.

◀ The dining space is composed simply of a wood table, metal chairs, and a few sentimental treasures displayed on a built-in shelving unit.

▶ A two-tiered pedestal dish made by Wendy and packed with strawberries, figs, and blueberries awaits Lolita's hungry appetite.

THE FAMILY ROOM IS staged with a few striking statement pieces. Its paint chipping away, an intricately carved French daybed (that also serves as the guest bed) centers beneath another of Fred's spectacular collages. By utilizing a discarded bed frame, he's created numerous compartments, individually framing heirloom pictures. The project is accompanied by foreign currency, again fastened to the wall with simple straight pins. In the corner, a tiny side table and metal chair offer additional seating and surface area for another of Wendy's incredible arrangements. Opposite the seating, an antique, blue, paint-chipped cupboard houses the television and is topped by a delicate strand of ceramic pieces, three glass bug catchers (used as vases), and a series of small treasure boxes. For a more vibrant feel, the large window is draped in a fuchsia sari that complements the room's hard elements and adds a touch of softness and warmth. Across from the window, a large gilded mirror serves to bounce light, expand the space, and provide depth. Picking up the shimmering tones of the sari, salvaged ceramic flowers are hung in a neat row above the mirror.

▲ **Across from the daybed, a well-worn cabinet shelters the television at eye level and provides more display surface for another of Wendy's artistic floral groupings.** *(inset)* **On one side of the TV cabinet, a cluster of antique glass boxes holds Indian bracelets and jewelry, treasures from a summer's vacation.**

▶ **A full-length antique mirror leans casually on one wall while porcelain flowers "hang to dry" in a line above.**

▶▶ **Though sun-bleached and slightly faded, these antique French flowers still add a spurt of color and life.**

◀ **With a few more splashes of color, the family room easily transitions into guest quarters.** *(inset top)* **Fred has used a bed frame and created the perfect frame, a smart solution for displaying his own collection of heirloom pictures.** *(inset bottom)* **This oversized arrangement brings life to an easily overlooked corner.**

▲ Luckily for Fred and Wendy, the kitchen came with these amazing pine cabinets. Clearly, their great storage space, functional prep surface, and rustic look further add to the old-world European style of the home.

▶ In the kitchen a large cutwork table and two open-back, bistro-style chairs create the family's informal dining space.

A GATHERING PLACE AT THE rear of the house, the kitchen holds many artistic creations and found objects. In place of modern cabinetry, an antique two-piece pine hutch has been installed. The effect is a powerful statement and an eye-catching conversation piece. Its functional countertop allows ample prep space, and its weathered exterior is childproof, as two-year-old Lolita often likes to help "cook." A round, metal-cutwork table and bistro-style chairs serve as a perfect spot for a quick bite. Although the refrigerator and sink are hidden in an adjoining pantry, Wendy and Fred have combined the two spaces by extending their collections of found-again European goods, including an iron crucifix, French pottery, and wooden dough bowls.

▲ Quite the little helper, Lolita prepares food with her pint-size pots and pans. A collection of antique hearts is grouped above the stove.

▼ A small alcove/pantry off the main room holds the sink and shelves of antique pottery and wooden dough bowls while a rusted, lacy metal cross adds striking contrast on the wall.

FORMERLY THE ATTIC, the second story has been divided in half with a room for Lolita and a master loft. The simple iron bed is easily dressed with a striped linen duvet and vintage white bedding. For temporary convenience, Lolita shares the space in an antique baby bed all her own, snuggled up to Mom's side. And at its base, an antique trunk provides storage and displays another of Wendy's masterpieces. A small, three-legged side table majestically crowned in citrus branches and sweeping ivy sits bedside for basic nightstand needs. Fred's imaginative and inspiring groupings of wall art continue upstairs to complete this space.

▲ As much as anywhere else in the home, the wall is a place to make statements. The combination of horizontally hung living plants and a series of vertically hung number plates give this corner of the master bedroom its own quiet but confident appeal.

◄ Casually made with mixed and matched linens, the master bed has an easy sort of elegance, while the vintage hotel sign on the wall brings a curious whimsy. *(inset)* A small, square, rusted table and wall ledge work together, serving as nightstand.

► A set of lockers becomes a dresser, concealing and sometimes shelving the family's clothes.

WATCHED OVER BY A HOVERING guardian angel and hand-made doll, Lolita's antique bassinet rests peacefully in a corner of her room. Originally a hospital supply stand, another found object has been revamped and is now used in place of the customary changing table. Interestingly enough, the pint-sized princess has a fascination with bugs and so Dad has fashioned an incredible mobile of (what else?) bugs that keeps Lolita occupied while changing. On an opposite wall, a meticulous, vintage collection of creepy crawlers has been fastened Lolita-height, and miniature shutter doors conceal Lolita's clothes.

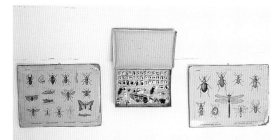

▲ *(top)* **To one side of the room an old hospital cabinet now works comfortably as a changing table and dresser for some of Lolita's things.** *(above)* **An unexpected but charming addition, an antique bug collection and a pair of labeled matching posters have been mounted child-height, on a wall.**

▶ **Fred takes Lolita's shoes from her pint-sized closet and attempts to explain why it's necessary to wear them.**

◀ **With flowing fabric and its very own guardian angel, Lolita's baby cradle looks as if it comes out of a fairy tale.**

A COMMON FEATURE of homes on hills is a compact tiered yard. The Testu's home is no exception. A multi-layered deck allows optimal use of given space. Another iron daybed fitted with cushy pillows and draped in mosquito netting, joined with a small table and chairs, provides an outdoor sanctuary overlooking Lolita's play area below.

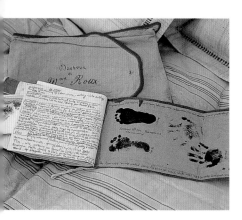

▲ *(top)* **Since it overlooks San Francisco, the deck is a favorite spot for evening dining.** *(above)* **A scrapbook of Lolita's first precious moments.**

▶ **In the backyard, Mom has fashioned a tepee from some branches and a piece of canvas, providing Lolita with her own hideaway.**

◀ **Another French daybed has been brought outside and dressed with mosquito netting, serving as comfy outdoor seating.**

A grand birdcage rests
snugly in a niche at the
stairway landing. A small
cluster of mini-potted
spruce adds a bit of warmth.

Style Tips

Wendy and Fred love, as they say, "junking." As newlyweds they used to go junking at flea markets every weekend, finding inspiration in old things. They still do! They also have local haunts they love to regularly explore. Here are some of their tips for finding things you love:

1 To avoid the wrong purchase, ask yourself, "Do I really need that?"

2 Before you buy something, know where it's going to go.

3 Don't be afraid to be creative—give things a new purpose.

4 When flea marketing, shop the entire flea market, look in all the booths; you never know what treasures you might find around the next corner.

Style Checklist

☑ Build on a fresh canvas of white.

☑ Sparely fill your space with sturdy, aged, French-feeling furnishings.

☑ Create innovative uses for old things: daybeds as sofas, a garden statue as indoor art, an old bed frame as a picture frame.

☑ Keep similar things together: photos, keys, eggs, antique pottery, bugs, etc.

☑ Find a budding artist (preferably you) and proudly display their artwork.

The antique corbels that work
into the gabled entry help make
a statement of uniqueness.
(inset) An array of Jane's nostalgic
collectibles sits in a weathered
yellow hutch off the kitchen.

CHAPTER TWO

Collectible Cottage

THE ADAMS FAMILY HOME

THROUGH THE DREAMY LANDSCAPE and up a winding mountain road lies the home of Jane, Robert, and Jesse Adams. A century old, the newly remodeled farmhouse overlooks the picturesque view of Marin County's Mount Tamalpais—a "view that feeds their souls." Hidden beneath a canopy of imposing shade trees, the formal cottage warmly welcomes its visitors.

Originally from Massachusetts (Robert) and Wisconsin (Jane), the duo began working together twenty years ago as museum-quality framers. However, after six years and the birth of their son, their common passion for craft artists and antiques took precedence with the opening of their home store, Summerhouse. Although Jane does not consider their home an "interior-designed home," the two have built up their personal collections through their travels and created a beautiful and unique style that we call *Collectible Cottage.*

The Adamses' latest obsession is Japanese culture. Consequently, anything related to the subject has come to be of prime importance to

The Adams family (from left): Robert, Jesse, and Jane.

▲ Abundant natural light pours in through a wall of open, unobstructed windows.

▶ An old store counter serves as a console table, displaying a colorful collection of wool blankets. An antique wicker rocker provides cozy seating.
(inset) An antique bridal crown hangs on the front door like a mini wreath.

(top right) The dining room, its entrance defined by huge French plant stands with blooming bougainvillea, houses a collection of mismatched chairs.

them. Between sixteen-year-old Jesse's Japanese-language lessons and family trips to San Francisco's Japan town, finding time to indulge their personal pastimes (Jane's gardening and antiquing, Robert and Jesse's fishing trips) can be difficult. Yet with Jane's inclination for delegation, or perhaps it's their attention to the concept of "full circle" (following through with everything one starts), they manage to seek out and find harmony in life.

Although a busy home schedule might overwhelm another group, the family remains undaunted, finding peace in frequent barbecues, potlucks, or serene sunsets—all enjoyed from their own yard. Their yard is of extreme importance to them as a place for meditation and therapeutic relaxation, and they have big plans for it. "We can't wait to complete the gardens. . . . We already spend hours potting plants . . . and want to add lots of huge stones." The stones would be for basking in the Bay Area sun or for meditation, not just for aesthetic appeal. Inside, the family (including the five cats) live in synchronization with the objects they have collected. "We don't worry about stuff; if it gets broken, it's meant to be." By selecting items that speak to their soul *and* pocketbook, the Adamses have created a look that is easily maintained and replenished. For Jane, a budget leads to increased creativity and a beautifully inspirational home.

COLLECTIBLE COTTAGE STYLE is like a scrapbook. Each page, each room is full of memories and collections from life's journeys. It is where home is a place that can make anyone feel comfortable and peaceful. From the moment you enter, the contents gently lull its occupants into reminiscent, nostalgic moods. And like every cottage, it's full of charm and nestled by nature. For the

Adamses, it's a sacred spot for quiet privacy and cherished family time.

TWO MASSIVE, ANTIQUE CORBELS flank the oversized front door, which opens wide to give one an eyeful of the home's primary living space: dining room, family room, and kitchen. Yet, instinctively, our eyes are drawn left to the gigantic antique French planters framing the dining room. From years of use, the original white paint has chipped away to reveal rust and wear, but the intricate detail of the cut-metal flowers remains beautifully intact. The dining room is surrounded by undraped windows and folding doors, allowing soft sunlight to spill in on the room's few contents—an antique table, a slatted bench, and mismatched chairs.

Suspended from the ceiling, a silk chandelier points toward the collection Jane has assembled beneath. She creates seasonal tablescapes from her vast collections—an antique santos bust, a vintage wooden bird, a pair of tapered candles, and a short stack of antique books topped with miniature Moroccan shoes—an alternative to a traditional centerpiece. Like the table and chairs, nothing "matches," but varied elements have been coordinated beautifully. This is a great option for those who don't have yards brimming with fresh flowers or the skill of a florist's touch.

The casualness of the dining room makes it the perfect spot to do homework.

PAST THE DINING ROOM the space opens into the living room, a somewhat long, narrow area. Robert and Jane used two jumbo antique columns to add width and to separate the room into two distinctive seating areas. The main space is chock-full of a variety of objects for wall and tabletop collections. While Jane primarily focuses her talent on tabletops, Robert tends to the walls by creating a tapestry of textures, colors, and subjects. Above the creamy white sofa topped in assorted ticking pillows, a grouping of vintage and antique still lifes downsize the large wall. For Robert, the value of each painting lies in the memory its purchase produced, not in the price paid. In other words, buy what you like!

◄ The living room is alive with fabric and textures, from the kilim rug to the Indian throw and striped mattress-ticking pillows. A pair of antique columns separates the long space into two distinct seating areas.

► In an alcove off the living room, this inspiring display combines mostly old with some new elements (a captivating painting of the sky), including another magnificent santos topped with a vintage flowered doll's hat.

THE RECENTLY REMODELED kitchen boasts the latest in appliances and functional storage solutions. However, the most intriguing and charming pieces are the series of one-of-a-kind collectibles. Even in their kitchen, Jane and Robert incorporate all the things they love. Small antique Buddhas overlook bowls of fruit, antique cream ware, and tiny sculptures made by close friends. The large clusters of monochromatic flowers add life, while such unexpected additions as the small boudoir lamp add whimsy and depth. We love how this family's approach is so carefree and unpredictable. Throw caution to the wind . . . make your own rules!

▲ Some of the Adamses' cherished objects—an antique creamer and Baby Jesus in a manger—bask in the sunlight.

◀ The updated and airy kitchen is stylish and functional. It shelters stacks of dishes, fruit bowls, and chopping blocks, among many other collectibles.

▶ The openness of the kitchen layout makes it easier for Jane and Jesse to talk while preparing salad for dinner.

THE FIRESIDE ROOM reestablishes the notion of "cottage." Slightly more shadowy, its warmer hues backdropped by the dark stone fireplace envelop its occupants. Tangible textures abound: down-stuffed pillows crowd the plush sofa and chairs while antique footstools, Jane's latest collectible obsession, cozy up to their bases. A floral theme continues throughout the home; while present mostly in this room, it adds a warm magic. Another predominant theme of the house, and in particular this space, is made with antique religious icons: santos, rosaries, crucifixes, etc. The tranquil intensity apparent in these pieces would add a measure of emotion to any décor. Mixtures of shapes and sizes of objects from times past lend themselves to memories of playing in Grandma's attic. Living with pieces from the past is key to the style of *Collectible Cottage*.

◀ **One of the Adamses' many santos, this one stands in its own peaceful corner, complete with candles and other treasures that create an altar-like feel.**

◀◀ **The fireside room showcases a dark brick fireplace behind antique parlor chairs, vintage still lifes, and numerous religious icons.**

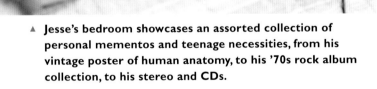

▲ Jesse's bedroom showcases an assorted collection of personal mementos and teenage necessities, from his vintage poster of human anatomy, to his '70s rock album collection, to his stereo and CDs.

▶ At the stairway landing, a timeworn cabinet is topped with a beautiful scrollwork frame. A much smaller painting is gently propped inside, embellished with a freshly snipped orchid and collectible accents.

OFF THE LANDING AT THE TOP of the stairs, Jesse's bedroom is a typical teenager's room in many ways—with a computer desk, television, video games, stacks of CDs and books—all the necessities essential for any sixteen-year-old-boy's room. The focal point is an awesome antique poster of the human anatomy that Jane was lucky enough to find in her travels abroad, doubling as a headboard for Jesse's bed. Simple blue-ticking linens and antique grain-sack pillows are style conscious but masculine, age appropriate but transitional. Instead of hiding away the electronics and his everyday mementos, Jesse has artfully displayed them throughout his room. Like father (or mother), like son!

THE MASTER AND GUEST BATHS are dreamscapes in and of themselves. Various refurbished Victorian doors, complete with delicate details of etched glass have replaced the previous and usual everyday doors. Free-standing sinks are paired with weathered wood mirrors framed by wall sconces. Quiet light spills from salvaged crystal chandeliers, and clusters of candles and bottles adorn small side tables and found shelves. Claw-foot tubs and vintage wicker chairs complete the scene, all set on floors of hand-laid mosaic tile. Although both rooms are similar in format, the distinct uniqueness that all of the recycled trimmings possess afford each a sense of individuality.

◄ Jesse's bath is classic cottage style, with the white pedestal sink, mosaic tiled floors, and oval beveled mirror. The hand-carved, etched-glass door is a pleasant surprise.

(top) The master bath (like Jesse's bath) features another etched glass door opening up to an idyllic spa-like retreat complete with an assortment of bottles filled with soothing herbal oils, soaps, and perfumes.

Collectible Cottage **43**

◄ **The master bedroom's classic white foundations—the walls and bed—allow space for vibrant additions, like the blue nightstand, its yellow counterpart, and floral bed linens. *(inset)* Jane hangs one of her crafted artisan pieces on the master bedroom door—which is a twin to the master bath door. *(below right)* A full-length golden mirror rests beside a wood dresser. Both statement pieces are adorned with collectible treasures, including a magnificent rosary hanging atop the mirror.**

▼ **Another santos, delicately adorned with an antique baby bonnet and bridal head garland, pensively gazes from a corner of the master bedroom.**

A VAULTED CEILING AND WALL of windows provide a feeling of open airiness and allow for a perfect view of the open mountainside. Yet, the master bedroom is sweet, romantic, cozy. Robert and Jane have filled their personal space with gifts they have given to each other. A fabulous, full-length gold mirror leaning informally against the wall sets off the tall walnut bureau and coordinating mirrored dresser. Two nightstands, one green, one blue, support a pair of matching aged lamps and more groupings of tangible memories. Across the antique-white rattan bed, layers of flowered linens continue their floral theme. At the base of the mirror a couple of antique pictures find a resting place. As with numerous other objects throughout the home, their placement is effortless and casual. That's what is so exciting about this type of design: you don't have to have a master plan. It's spontaneous—just do it!

WHILE THE LANDSCAPING is a work in progress, the home has many balconies lush with potted plants, as well as Adirondack and wicker furniture.

▲ **The Adamses enjoy their incredible view and a few precious moments at day's end.**

▶ **At the foot of the stairs a corner table holds sentimental heirlooms.**

Style Tips

Clearly the Adamses have an incredible talent. Jane says it's exciting to shop for collections because "now you have something to hunt for." The two look at buying as a game—setting a budget and sticking to it. Anyone can furnish a house in three days, but it takes a lifetime to personalize it. Consequently, the Adamses are still on the hunt. When asked for advice, Jane and Robert offered the following tips for finding those special treasures to personalize your home:

1 There are treasures everywhere. Don't be discouraged with your location—just get out there and look.

2 Try asking antiques dealers where they go to shop.

3 Don't give up if you miss out or pass on a good deal. There's always "the one that got away."

4 Have fun—shopping is a great way to relax or hang out with friends.

Style Checklist

✔ Gather together your collections and keep collecting.

✔ Display against neutral backdrops of white, cream, and beige.

✔ Compose tablescapes and wallscapes by combining various elements from your collections.

✔ Utilize old materials in new designs. Some Adams family examples are: using old doors to replace original ones, hanging corbels as a front-door embellishment, and using pillars to separate seating areas in the living room.

The "Remade" Burch home in the Phoenix desert sun.

Remade Ranch

THE BURCH FAMILY HOME

IN THE HEART OF OLD-TOWN Phoenix, hidden in a lush green pocket within a grove of 100-year-old olive, citrus, and towering pecan trees, lies a soothing oasis. Shrouded by tropical vines, plush lawns, sweeping palms, and shaded verandas, the home exudes a peaceful, relaxing aura that can be felt from outside. Beyond its exotic gardens and through the ominous front door, the sense of serenity continues, restful and calm. The space is full of warm light and cool colors. This fabulously renovated and absolutely comfortable dwelling is the handsome home of Brian, Beverly, Alex, and Emily Burch.

With an almost otherworldly, resort-like feel, the Burch home is a blur of action. The perpetual summertime climate of Arizona makes outdoor living essential. So, in their house renovation, the extension of inside to the outside was a major priority. As Brian coaches Little League, Bev enjoys gardening, Alex (twelve) practices golf and Emily (nine) performs gymnastics, clearly the yard is their family's living area. When they are not swimming in the pool or bouncing on the trampoline, the

**The Burch Family Portrait (from left):
Emily, Brian, Alex, and Bev.**

49

Burches enjoy traveling to the beach and attending family get-togethers. Through practical design and thoughtful arrangements, the home's furnishings hold up well to numerous activities. From roller-skating in the halls to school projects strewn across the dining table or kitchen counter, hardwood floors provide a sturdy and durable foundation. Actually, the Burches' greatest challenge has not been spills or scuffs but the construction phase of the family's home project. "We ran out of wood three times and then demolition stopped construction for six months!" said Bev. The result, though, was an elegant space with room to spare and abounding comfort. For the Burches, it's home; for the rest of us, it's simply quite lovely.

Though currently just Alex and Emily skate about the halls, the Burch tribe extends well beyond its youngest members; this close-knit family boasts six children, four in-laws, and six grandchildren. After years of cozy gatherings, it became apparent that a more adequate space was needed. So, five years ago Brian and Bev began the work of transforming their historic ranch-style home into a sprawling, light-filled space with room to spare. The end product was an impressive estate reminiscent of an Italian- or Spanish-style villa. Following the remodel, Bev started to fill her "new" space with functional furnishings and classic accessories. Through the process she discovered an ability for design that resulted in opening a lifestyle store of her own. By combining "littles" (what Bev calls whimsical chatchkas) with bits of modern and vintage trims, she has created a look that is simple but exceedingly stylish. It's an individualized desert take on the metropolitan home, and we've called it *Remade Ranch*.

WHAT IS REMADE RANCH? It's the conscious incorporation of the outside's wide-open space that's peppered with growths of trees and carpeted in luscious lawns. It's grand yet casual. It's spacious but intimate. It's creating rooms within rooms through purposeful arrangement, designating functional vignettes for conversation. It's careful attention to detail and the modern application of timeworn pieces meticulously blended with sentimental touches.

◄ **A whimsical vase allows white Gerber blooms their natural graceful posture.**

◄◄ **Off the courtyard entry, the lush side garden with a babbling fountain is "magical in the springtime when it's full of hummingbirds," according to Bev.**

THE LIVING ROOM GLOWS, as bowing palm fronds peek in through the gigantic, nearly twenty-foot-high wall of windows. Except for a handful of pastels, the room is radiantly decked in white-on-white, and at its middle, four armless scroll-back chairs surround a tailored linen ottoman. Stacks of books and an antique milk-glass vase (from Bev's father's collection) transform the slipcovered piece from an oversized footstool into a trendy upholstered tabletop. Down-filled, sun-faded floral pillows complete the scene and increase a sense of soft easiness. Desiring to create a different look for the home's focal point (the living room), Bev chose this seating arrangement, slipcovering all the pieces for a dramatic statement, kid-proofing, and durability. The individual seating also frees up floor space, giving the room a greater sense of openness, while precariously stacked books decrease any feel of formality. Beyond this vignette at the wall of windows, an antique French-style table and rattan chairs, framed by two pairs of salvaged pillars, continue the white palette, reflecting the desert sun.

▲ **An arched doorway framed in weathered blue shutters leads to a side garden with a bubbling fountain.**

◄ **Through smart design techniques the massive living room still feels cozy and intimate, with an oversized ottoman surrounded by four scroll-back chairs, creating a conversation center.**

One seating area in the family room combines a white denim-slipped sofa with an unexpected black leather chair facing the room's entertainment center. *(inset)* A second seating area in the family room nestles in front of the fireplace. A stack of wicker trunks becomes a side table while a low, antique pine trunk serves as a coffee table. An area rug provides warmth and defines the space.

THE FAMILY ROOM IS more of a living space. This "Great Room" is separated into functional and distinct seating areas allowing for separate but connected gathering spots. This is Bev's favorite room. With such a large family, the ability to congregate in a common space while maintaining the possibility for different conversations "is a true blessing." By carefully mixing linen, floral prints, leather, and weathered wood, she has created diverse sections that complementarily flow into one another. A white denim sectional and leather-studded chair sit comfortably in front of the entertainment unit, while a brocade loveseat and vintage floral armchairs cozy up fireside. A large, round, pedestal dining table that can easily seat ten rests below the vintage and attentive gaze of *Christ's Last Supper*. In a back corner, a large glass door opens onto the room's extension. The covered patio full of cushioned antiques and a glass-topped tin table further enhance this family room, allowing for the enjoyment of lazy Arizona nights.

▲ This casual dining space is where the family spends most of its mealtimes. A reproduction hutch showcases some of Bev's favorite dishes.

(top) A great alternative to a scrapbook, two antique glass-lidded jars hold a small collection of books and corks, encapsulating some of the Burch family's most momentous occasions.

▶ As the extended family room, this covered patio is home to an old painted wood cross, iron daybed acting as a sofa, a tin-topped table, and variously colored wicker and metal rockers and chairs.

- **The simple brick arch sets the mood of the kitchen, classic ranch with a contemporary edge shown in the stainless-steel appliances and black granite countertop.**

- **One of Bev's favorite found objects, this altarpiece offers a dramatic backdrop to a vase of garden flowers.**

WHILE STILL PART OF the family room, the kitchen is a markedly separate spot. Sharp contrasts of white, black, and stainless steel are brought together beneath a used-brick archway. Modern appliances are softened by flea market finds and antique "littles." On the countertop an original altarpiece holds a vintage chalice and spray of garden flowers, while a glass garden cloche serves as a cheese dome. At the counter's end, two wrought-iron barstools with curved backs add an element of romance, as the entire space comes together beautifully below a tin-tiled ceiling.

THE HARDWOOD FLOORS, peaked ceiling, muted tones, and plump cushions combine to give the master bedroom a sleepy elegance. Two mismatched but well-coordinated, white-slipped armchairs flank the four-poster bed. At its foot, a pine Irish hope chest acts as a surface for incense, books, and a splash of color. In place of the expected nightstands, they have chosen a small antique desk for Bev and a larger one for Brian. She neatly stores magazines and other reading materials in baskets beneath her desk; his is piled high with stacks of books. Bev tells us with a smile, "He requires just a bit more space than I do." But more than its beautiful furnishings, the room's most appealing asset is the stained-glass family tree, an incredible surprise for Brian and Bev designed by their home's architect. Just off the room's main space, the master bath is surrounded by windows that overlook Bev's herb garden. Seashells, orchids, and romantic candlelight create a mood for bubble baths and dreamy bliss.

▲ **The master bath overlooks the vegetable and herb garden, as well as the koi pond.**

◄ **The master bedroom, dressed in shades of white with just a touch of sage green and antique pine, is a peaceful retreat for the parents of six children.** *(inset)* **Bev's nightstand provides the essentials: a dimly lit lamp, an ample supply of reading material, and the fabulous Burch family portrait.**

► **At about four in the evening, the stained-glass family tree comes to life, casting dabbles of pinks and blues throughout the room, a constant and everlasting reminder of their treasured family legacy.**

A FAN OF MYTH, LEGEND, and boyhood fantasies, Alex chose a décor that harkens back to a time of chivalrous knights and courageous battles. The oriental rug, darkened furniture, and large wood-slat blinds evoke feelings of warmth that this naturally shady room otherwise would not have. Alex is quite the collector himself and proudly displays his artifacts throughout his space. Salvaged traffic signs leaning at the foot of the bed add a punch of color and mix well with tiny details such as the wooden beaded rosary hanging on the headboard. On an open and freestanding shelving unit, the meticulously stacked cigar boxes backdrop numerous Lego creations and members of his action-figure collection.

▲ A shelving unit supports the fruits of twelve-year-old Alex's labor, including Lego pirate ships, Star Wars fighters, and countless others. His stereo, layered cigar-box collection, and wire baskets holding sports equipment keep Alex entertained and organized.

◄ Alex's room features objects of fun, fantasy, and function, from his whimsical traffic signs to his antique sword collection. *(inset)* A simple beaded rosary hangs bedside.

► Style meets function: Alex's room still allows him room to play with one of his flying creations.

▲ A vintage coat rack, "Emily-height," offers easy access and kid-friendly organization. *(above right)* Beaded shades top this three-arm sconce over Emily's bed, surrounded by a canopy of glow-in-the-dark stars.

◄ Emily's princess canopy bed trimmed in floral garlands and topped with pink ballet slippers promises sweet dreams. *(inset top)* Besides books, Emily's bedside bookshelf holds dolls, tea sets, and even a pair of pink boots. Can you tell what her favorite color is? *(inset bottom)* Perfect for tea parties and dress-up, this seating area at the foot of the bed, with a floral-slipped loveseat and white trunk full of costumes, hosts many make-believe gatherings.

► Like mother, like daughter—Emily playing hostess.

▼ Emily's bath is soft and sweet in complementary sage-green accents.

EMILY'S ROOM IS TIED UP in hues of mellow pink and dusty rose. Fit for any princess, the canopy-style bed is dressed in pink flowers and white rosebuds. And though the walls are white, they have been dusted with a myriad of glow-in-the-dark stars and soft, yellow light from the vintage three-arm sconce topped in small beaded shades. A shelving unit—bookcase style—houses dolls, teapots, books, and the necessities for dress-up at one side. On another, a small upholstered settee and white-wash chest provide the perfect setup for a tea party. Bev has incorporated both adult-size furniture (settee, bed) and child-size pieces (table, chairs, coat rack) to make the space inviting for all ages. As every girl desires her own dressing space, Emily is lucky enough to have a perfect powder room, complete with a crystal chandelier. Cool accents and tile work in celadon green offset the predominantly white theme set by a reproduction wooden vanity.

WHILE THE HOUSE SITS on a spacious lot, cozy vignettes designate spots of special interest. On one side of the yard, a cottage-like potting shed nestles in its corner, heavily shaded by large pecan trees. Brick patios are lined with raised flowerbeds, while hedges and vine-covered walls border the perimeter. By using salvaged doors, the gateways give the yard an even softer, more personalized feeling. Throughout the yard, Bev has incorporated such old or salvaged pieces as flowerpots, wooden troughs, statuary, and architectural elements.

▲ **A blue wood trough is the perfect storage place (or hiding place) for a garden hose.**

◄ **A potting table is lined in old birdhouses, aged terra-cotta pots, and rustic toolboxes just right for garden tools. A blue bicycle with a flower-filled basket waits for an afternoon ride.**

► **Bev steals a quiet moment for herself on a veranda off the master bedroom. Spaces like this make the home even more charming.**

▲ Alex and Emily lace up. Like Bev says, "This is a true family house where my kids really do skate down the halls."

▶ Old French canisters hold bath supplies and add a delicate floral motif.

Style Tips

By broadly mixing vastly different styles, the Burches have created a cohesive and distinctive look. It is functional, family friendly, and elegant but maintains a graceful sophistication. For Bev, it's easy—she simply looks for what she calls the "WOW factor." To help capture the feeling of *Remade Ranch*, Bev provided the following tips:

1 Look for things that have a story, character, or a challenge.

2 Don't get stuck in style genres; mix new with old, modern with classic, etc.

3 Buy your staple furniture pieces new—the accents (the "littles") can be old.

4 Buy your upholstered pieces slipcovered.

Style Checklist

✔ Start with white staples: sofas, chairs, tables, cabinets.

✔ Combine new furnishings with old statement pieces for a mixture of durability, functionality, and rustic style.

✔ Use unexpected accents to bring in small touches of color and contrast. Some Burch family examples are: shutters framing doorways, black leather chairs, stacks of books, milk-glass accessories.

✔ Create intimate spaces within rooms by arranging furnishings in conversation centers and cozy vignettes.

✔ Utilize the outdoors and extend living spaces onto porches and patios.

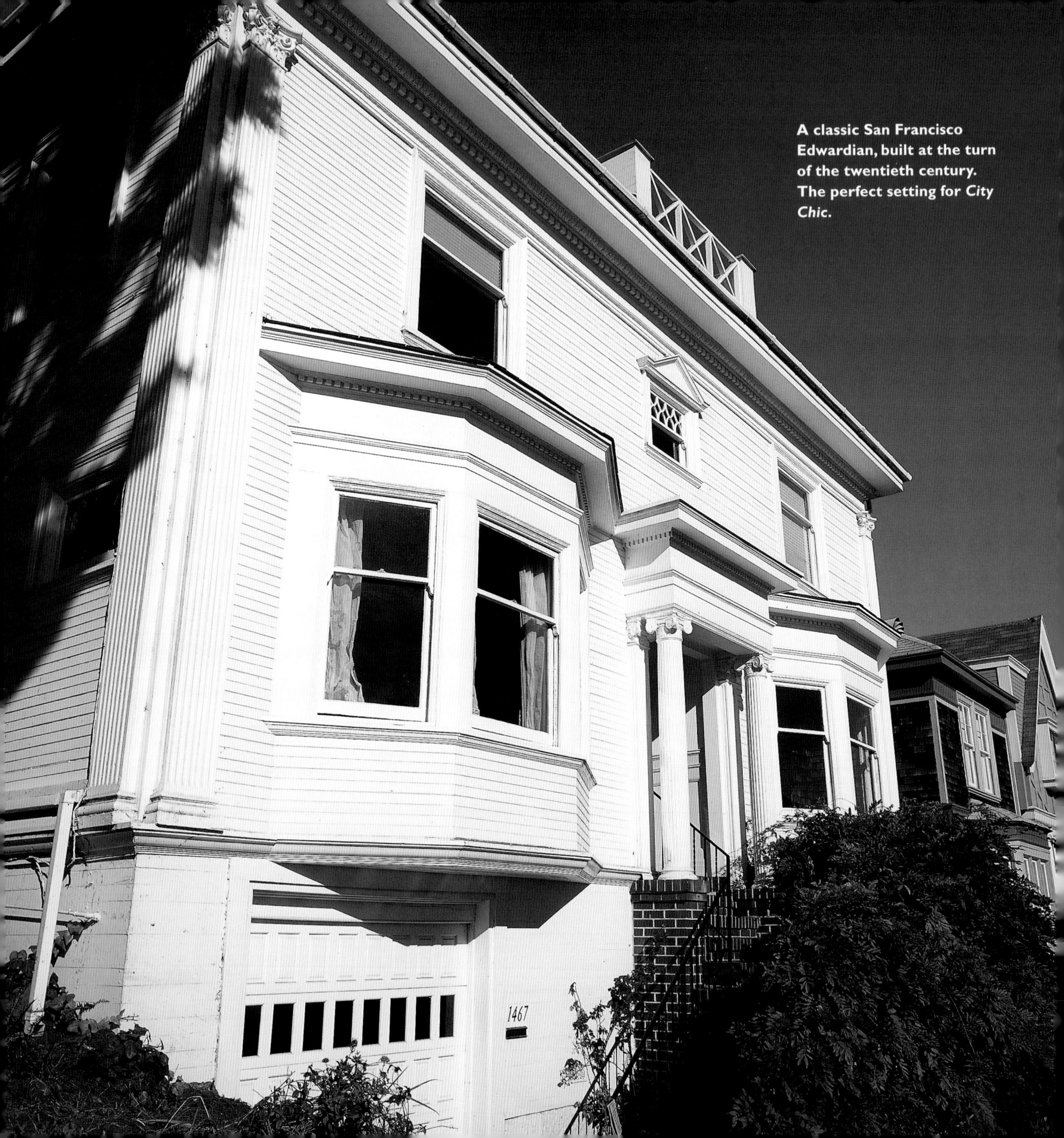

A classic San Francisco Edwardian, built at the turn of the twentieth century. The perfect setting for *City Chic*.

1467

CHAPTER FOUR

City Chic

THE OBEROI FAMILY HOME

NIMA OBEROI WAS BORN and raised in a small suburb of New Delhi, India. Coming to the States as a wide-eyed, impressionable young woman, she founded Lunares, an industry-leading wholesale company. Her career has provided an outlet for her innate creativity and love for design; but most of all, it has brought her joy. And with the recent purchase of a fantastic San Francisco estate, Nima and the rest of her family, along with Sophy, her best friend from childhood, have been able to incorporate business savvy into the making of a warm, comfortable, sensual abode. This space is definitely *City Chic*.

Nima's passion for cooking and entertaining family and close friends was one of the most important factors in choosing her home. "The space had to feel stylish but informal—ideal for dinner parties and just hanging out!" she says. It was bought and decorated, keeping this lifestyle of relaxed, fashionable living in mind. Every room is meant not only for Nima's enjoyment but also for that of her constant houseful of guests and her cocker spaniel, Cosmo. In fact, our consummate hostess

Cosmo and Nima on the porch.

69

▲ Nima's bird candleholders make a graceful table display. The natural variations of the shadow box beneath offer the perfect backdrop.

▲ Piles of books and a small cluster of Moroccan tea glasses are collected atop this shard console table; a large glass jug with willow branches and a modern magnifying lamp also demand attention.

▶ A ceramic tea set adorns a shadow-box-like table displaying some of nature's vivid beauties.

▶▶ The entry console with its sleek, vibrant display radiates against the kiwi green backdrop. The glowing nest of light above offers a natural, though unexpected contrast. *(inset)* Cleverly disguised behind layers of twigs and moss, and dripping with crystal pendants, the entry hall's light fixture has been dramatically transformed into a functional, affordable conversation piece.

admits that once a room is done, she sleeps in it for a month or two to make sure everything is comfortable and just right. Each space comes outfitted with clean lines, low, comfy furniture, and a great deal of whimsy, all trademarks of this city dweller's signature style. And when she's not entertaining or globetrotting, she's out in the garden (which, she claims, is more therapeutic than cooking because "there's no guilt involved"). She laughingly admits, "I've always been a freak about gardens. I can remember when I was seventeen in India; I would sneak clippings from neighborhood gardens and cultivate them in my own. I had a fabulous garden there, and this one, which is still a work in progress, will eventually be fabulous too!" Inside or out, Nima has created an accommodating abode that is smooth and sassy—fabulous indeed!

An impressive and stately residence, Nima's home sits austerely atop a steep hill in one of San Francisco's oldest and most notable communities. The classic Edwardian home, built more than one hundred years ago, is clearly a crowning jewel of the neighborhood. And although its time-honored straight lines and white columns might at first suggest a predictable, traditional interior, the design that Nima has created within is an unexpected blend of a bit of modern, just a dash of whimsy, and a whole lot of sexy.

SOPHISTICATED AND DARING, *City Chic* is a powerful combination of intense color punches and dramatic texture variations. It's a space that blends straight lines, angles, and plush fabrics in rooms of statement pieces. It is knowing when a single classic antique can create a focal point amid a sharp contrast of contemporary additions and modern accents. It's bold, uninhibited, and

very happy. In a space that is *City Chic*, your spirit is lifted and you can almost hear the laughter in the design . . . no, in the furnishings . . . no, it's in the place itself.

UP A FLIGHT OF STAIRS and through the front door, the immediate impression is one of grandeur. However, the large entry hall is simply decorated. The original dark wood trim has been preserved, contrasting with stark white walls. A grouping of monochromatic flowers in chunky aluminum vases is stunningly placed atop the straight lines of a black console table. Two frameless square mirrors pop off the vivid kiwi-green backdrop, hinting at the intensity to be found throughout the rest of the home. And yet, possibly the most interesting detail is found hovering above: instead of the existing ordinary fixture (this being one of the few rooms in the home without an original chandelier), Nima has created a work of art by simply covering it with "twigs" and a sporadic disbursement of crystals—totally chic!

▲ Nima's vivid color assortment of silks and satins pops against the dark furnishings and stark white walls.

◄ The living room is a feast of color, texture, and sensual lines.

► The Japanese-inspired tea table, surrounded by silk and satin floor cushions, serenely sits beneath unique leaded-glass windows.

▼ On the mantel, family photos backdrop a series of assorted candleholders, accented by leaves, flowers, and stark willow branches.

A PAIR OF MASSIVE POCKET DOORS opens to reveal the main parlor, or living room—and it's quite impressive. A stark white space is filled with the light of many detailed leaded windows. Increasing this light, a pair of huge, black-framed mirrors leans against the walls at the end of the room and serve to expand the space. Between and at their bases, a low glass-top table bordered by large silk floor pillows functions as a gathering place or a delicious spot for afternoon tea. But the room hinges on a personally designed sofa and matching chaise. Both straight-lined and ebony-stained, they overflow with fiery clusters of cushy silk pillows and warm fur throws. Set atop a cowhide rug and accompanied by two mirrored cubes, or coffee tables, the seating tempts guests and friends to take off their shoes, cozy up, and stay awhile. Sheltered beneath a large willow branch, an angular mantel tops the fireplace, supporting an intricate collection of candlesticks.

NIMA SAYS THIS STYLE is "not profound." And the dining room might be seen as an example of this. It's quite basic—a table and chairs surrounded by white walls. But what a magnificent table and chairs they are. Nima has designed an ebony-stained shadow box dining table that has been compartmentalized and filled with brilliantly colored natural elements: green moss, river rock, dried bamboo, preserved cornflowers, etc. The result is a dining table of function and fabulous form. A true socialite, Nima is always entertaining. As a solution to a perpetual demand for more seating, she's opted for a combination of dining chairs and benches fitted with leather green cushions that make for easy cleanup. In the background, a shallow closet accommodates neat rows of colorful glassware that reflect the colors in the table and serve as impromptu artwork.

▲ **Simply set white-on-white dinnerware and linen napkins, along with silvery accents, add contemporary sophistication.**

◄ **The dining room's sheer simplicity serves its purpose as Nima hosts gatherings with members of her extended family. The smart, oversized square table with alternating benches and chairs seats up to sixteen.**

► **The consummate hostess, Nima makes everyone feel at home.**

COOL AND CLEAN, THE KITCHEN is truly the heart of Nima's home. The "green" started here in this room. Complementing basic-white cabinets, contrasting black-granite countertops, and contemporary stainless-steel accents, the green was inspired by springtime. It's a happy new color; for Nima, color is an accessory "like an earring"—easily changeable. By limiting the colors of accessory pieces and painting just one primary wall, she has been able to inexpensively and easily create the illusion of a theme in her home without its usual con-strictiveness. Like she told us, "When I'm ready for a change, all I have to do is repaint this wall and I can have a whole new look!" To anchor the room as well as provide additional counter space, a stainless steel work-table with leather-topped stools also becomes a meeting spot for get-togethers, discussions, and cherished moments with friends.

▲ The kitchen sink overlooks the garden, while goldfish in a giant glass vase bask in the soft sunlight.

◄ Nima tells us her kitchen is quite basic: "black and white at its core" with only one wall and leather-topped stools in her trademark kiwi green.

► Bounding glass compotes hold colorful fruit in a small kitchen niche.

FITTED IN THE TINY NICHE beneath the staircase, a former coat closet has been transformed into a wash closet. Metallic silver paint lends itself to an illusion of larger space. In addition, an oversized mirror has been hung on the largest wall to add depth, while a tiny antique oval mirror adds alluring detail.

▲ The compact guest bath has been enlarged with silver metallic paint and an oversized mirror.

▶ While the home is primarily contemporary in its décor, traditional touches like this European wash-closet sign recall a past era.

◀ Nima's bedroom, simple and sparse, makes a powerful statement befitting this small-business powerhouse.

THE MASTER SUITE IS equipped with the bare essentials and a few luxurious details. A massive black bed is dressed in a combination of textures: an Egyptian cotton duvet, leather-fringed pillows, a silk bolster, and an antique linen coverlet. A nightstand, supporting an open-weave sofa, beaded table lamp, and a vase of long-stemmed roses, is laden with stacks of books at its base and lends surface area for personal items. Except for the armchair and large ottoman, the room is necessarily bare to reduce competition between its furnishings.

- ◄ The white leather headboard in the guest bedroom becomes a piece of art that quietly cooperates with the room's vibrant photographic collection.

- ► Two small aluminum stools scoot up to a low shelf running the length of the room. In addition to various collectibles, the shelf also holds a TV and VCR.

- ▼ A built-in window seat offers comfortable reading accommodations.

NIMA SOUGHT TO CREATE a space that would embody her love for the tradition and culture of her homeland. Inspired by lively pictures of a family celebration and incorporating Indian textiles, the guestroom is shocking in its vibrancy but completely welcoming in its appeal. The beautiful jewel tones splashed on a canvas of white echo India's romance with the celebration of life. A large bolster-type pillow fashioned from one of Nima's Indian shawls rests at a slight angle. Opposite the modern, leather headboard and platform bed, a low wall shelf has been affixed, running the length of the room; it displays all sorts of treasures and articles of interest as well as an entertainment/video station for younger guests. The window seat in the corner adds a sense of intimacy and a cozy spot to read a book on a foggy San Francisco day.

▲ A niche of shelves provides ample storage for Nima's work and personal mementos, while an ordinary easel brings an easily overlooked picture to the forefront.

▶ The workspace, a glorious tribute to light and color, is topped by Nima's own exquisite crystal-draped chandelier. The room is personalized with framed family photos covering walls and lining shelves, providing her with constant inspiration.

THE WORKSPACE IS CHEERFUL, bright, and totally functional. A large white table, placed directly in the center of the room and used as a work surface, desk, computer console, etc., is highlighted by another of Nima's creations. She transformed a common five-arm chandelier by draping it with countless strands of glittering crystal beads and individual deep red and amber crystal pendants; it is truly the centerpiece of this room. The remaining space is utilized by a series of wall shelves for display of found objects and labeled boxes that help keep her organized.

THE GARDEN IS A LITTLE piece of heaven. The small space is crowded with a mixture of thriving, blossoming greenery. The multileveled yard is divided by a series of ancient blue-mosaic-tiled stairways and lined with meandering sweet pea and herbs that culminate in a small vignette, the perfect setting for a glass of wine and a quick bite.

◀ Amid the luxurious overgrowth of aging shrubs, Cosmo and Nima take a break from the busy day and its grueling schedule.

▲ The calm respite of this garden is accented with original blue mosaic tiles and wandering herbs and ivies.

◄ On a shelf in the office, tiny treasures are liberally displayed.

▼ Cosmo sits patiently, awaiting his daily walk.

Style Tips

Nima is a shopper by nature. She loves to buy expressive things that reflect her personality. She finds sensuality in her home but most of all feels that it's a place of relaxed comfort and happiness. She shops anywhere she can find what she loves and what inspires her. Some of her tips for finding these things are:

1 Think outside of the box—open your mind to new things.

2 If it's a small piece, get a bunch of them and start a collection to make a statement.

3 Venture out—always be on the lookout for new places to shop.

4 There's no such thing as bad form—just bad application.

Style Checklist

☑ Begin with a black-and-white core: white walls, black furnishings.

☑ Use vibrant accessories to add splashes of sassy color.

☑ Blend an assortment of textures: silk and satin pillows, leather cushions, shiny metal accessories, wood furnishings.

☑ Maintain a consistency of straight lines throughout: architecture, furnishings, etc.

☑ Incorporate an unexpected statement and touches of glamour in lighting and painted backdrops. Some examples from Nima's home are crystal chandeliers and kiwi-green walls.

The 1850s mirror from a San Francisco estate reflects the antique clown costume that hides a less interesting door, opposite.

Romantic Renaissance

THE ADDISON FAMILY HOME

SHOPPING FOR VINTAGE clothes, taking in a movie or play, or just enjoying a dinner out—for the Addisons (Wendy and Monica, along with kitties Tristan and Sigfreid) time together is rare, so the shared moments and "girls'-night outings" are cherished. These two intensely creative individuals spend most of their time involved in their personal obsessions. For Wendy, "playing" in the work studio of their Theatre of Dreams shop or at flea markets are both occupation and fun, while Monica (fifteen) is consumed with theater productions and art direction. And like their passions, their home is a canvas that they are constantly reworking. In spite of its small size, houseguests are frequent, so the space is necessarily in a state of constant change. By rolling out/around various small pieces of furniture or fabric, they create rooms within the room. The TV, for example, is set on a rolling cart, that in essence, creates a "screening room" wherever it goes. Similarly, the lush garden transitions seasonally. Wendy notes that "in the wintertime it's a beautiful 3-D space to look at, and in the summer it turns

The Addison women (from left): Monica and Wendy stand in front of their home and workshop—Theatre of Dreams.

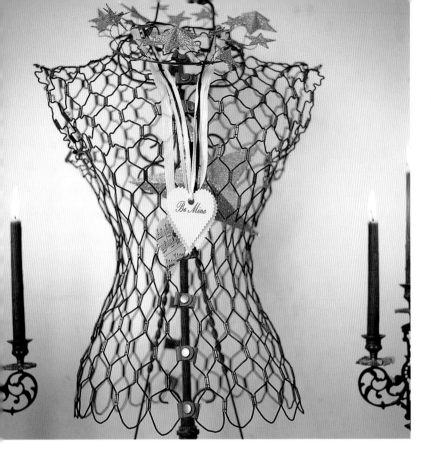

◄ A vintage wire mannequin is decked in Wendy's paper hearts.

(bottom left) **Wendy goes through her paper supplies, neatly organized in an original tin-lined humidor.**

▼ An antique Japanese silk robe hangs from the screen. (And, yes, Wendy does wear it!) On the other side is one of her first creations—a paper cone container made from sheet music, circa 1850, titled "**What Fairy Likes Music.**"

into a magical living room—all fenced in and private." Compact and cozy, the Addison home is proof that great things really do come in small packages.

Their home is located on a tranquil and shady shore of San Francisco's East Bay, where the hills part for a quiet clearing, in the tiny and slightly obscure community of Port Costa—truly another world. However, the miniature town, little more than its main road, is full of enchanting buildings and captivating homes. Here, amid the historic construction, one-lane roads, and imaginative townsfolk, Wendy and Monica set up Theatre of Dreams and tenderly fashioned a dreamscape of their very own.

Since childhood Wendy has "immersed herself in the past." It was a refuge for her, and consequently, she continues to hold a soulful attraction for it. Originally from St. Louis, Wendy came to the Bay Area twenty years ago armed with a consummate ability to create. Several years later and following the birth of her daughter Monica, she moved to Port Costa. For the Addisons there is magic in the past and stories to be uncovered. Through their unparalleled ability to feel this magic and hear these stories, Wendy and Monica collectively combine found treasures and tossed-aside materials to compose a nostalgically dreamy style, a *Romantic Renaissance*.

HAVE YOU EVER WANTED TO step back in time to a place where imagination and creativity prevail? To appreciate the enchantment and mystery of a past era? To be surrounded in muted tones dimly lit by oil lamps and glowing candles? This is *Romantic Renaissance*. It's the appreciation of old adorned objects, remnants, and scraps in a beautiful new way. It is careful attention paid to the innate function of items, elements, and materials, restoring them to their intended use. It's a whisper of simplicity with open-back chairs, gauzy fabrics, and smoky mirrors blending into feelings of vague familiarity and fairy-like fantasy.

UNLIKE A TRADITIONAL HOME, the Addisons' amazing front doors (salvaged from a local nineteenth-century convent) open not into a living room or entryway but instead into the Theatre of Dreams workshop. The small space is piled high with Wendy's recently procured objects from the past. The space is so breathtakingly full of both her collections and creations that you almost don't know where to look first. On one wall an antique clown costume is displayed, while another presents a weathered and aged forty-eight-star American flag. In a corner, a small table supports an incredible diorama, a dollhouse sculpture of sorts that is so detailed an adequate description would necessarily continue for several pages. But it is a large, antique, glass-door hutch and its abundant contents that designate the room's most interesting spot. Here, Wendy spends hours crafting her miraculous inventions from the boxes of vintage and antique materials she has collected and meticulously stored in individually labeled, old-fashioned cigar boxes. An aesthetic and practical method for storing any small goods, Wendy layers them for a visually stimulating effect.

The building, virtually divided in half, conceals its living quarters in the rear. Through a small and inconspicuous doorway, we are transported from the magic of the front workspace into the back living space. It has a scent of mystery and intrigue. In the shadows of one

A gauzelike piece of scrim drapes the dining table, with fresh ivy vines adding life and romance.

▶ *(top)* Below a framed antique theatrical flyer, a vintage wire mannequin is decked in Wendy's paper hearts.
(middle) A simple puddle of the draped tablecloth adds an element of drama.
(bottom) The open and airy kitchen provides ample prep space on the rolling, marble-top island, which holds an impressive coffee can collection below.

Wendy says of her home, "It's like walking into a place from your imagination."

◀ A bedside table provides subtle light and a picturesque backdrop.

▶ A glass-domed figurine is captured forever in all her splendor.

cozy main room (not including Monica's) the Addisons' entire home has come together.

INSTEAD OF BEING RESTRICTED by its openness and size, this family room additionally encompasses a bedroom, kitchen, and dining space. At one side, a massive window overlooking the garden is thinly draped by two sheer panels. The oversized portal filters light as it enters the room, casting shadows about the kitchen. This side of the room, focused more on practicality, centers around an antique store counter that Wendy has sensibly topped with old Carrera marble. Acting as prep space, the pseudo island increases counter surface and has storage underneath, and it provides an impromptu dining spot. Hovering above is one of the first pieces in Wendy's oil lamp collection. Fundamental to this design concept, the fixture is not just aesthetically pleasing; it is actually used as a lamp.

THE FORMAL DINING TABLE is really not formal at all. A small bistro table is dramatically clothed in cascades of gauzy material, while freshly cut snippets of ivy flow about the base of a pair of antique candleholders and a timeworn, glass-domed figurine. The intense setting is offset by a gilded 1850s mirror. As an attempt to soften its straight, rigid lines, Wendy added more trails of ivy, misted with gold spray paint, around its frame. While the scene is remarkably passionate, it possesses a comforting old-world hospitality that makes you want to sit, to stay. A quick spin (literally) and you're in the bedroom. A canopy of antique Japanese silk has been added to a simple French daybed. The result is delightfully dreamy. White-on-white lace bedding is neatly tucked and contrasted by an original Victorian tinsel painting.

▲ **Monica lounges, chatting on the phone with a friend.**

◀ **Monica's room speaks to her creative personality. Not afraid of color or content, she has filled the space with all the things she loves.**

▼ **Plucked from a junk store, this dresser displays some of Monica's favorites: her Mom's own series of paper boxes, a hand-painted wire-framed mask, and a vintage jacket with embroidered flowers.**

A die-cut 1880s folding screen (given to Wendy as a gift) increases privacy and frames this section of the room. To the side of the daybed an antique sewing machine doubles as a console table. Wendy has placed a vintage wire form and two candelabras with scattered bits of coral on its top and hung one of her "glittery letters" and an old theatrical newspaper clipping in a basic black frame. The area evokes an almost religious sacredness that is increased by the pure light of yet another oil lamp from her collection.

MONICA'S ROOM IS LIKE a collage, a layering of old cartoons, rock posters, and vintage 1940s chic; it's the manifest consciousness of a creative fifteen-year-old girl. Like her mom, Monica has begun collections of her own. Of these collections—paintings from friends—offer the perfect backdrop for her mixture of modern and vintage 1940s furnishings. Clothing is an integral part of this design concept. Vintage dresses are displayed throughout the room as works of art. The space is plush with soothing fabrics in deep colors, perpetuating a kind of spirited and soulful mood.

OUTSIDE, THE MOOD SHIFTS again as we enter another space . . . world . . . place of the imagination. This secret garden is a spot of deep inspiration. Small, winding brick paths are shrouded with lush vegetation. The area feels wild and untamed; Wendy admits to "gardening" but twice a year. Birdbaths and weathered statuary pieces increase the "faraway" feel of the yard. And in a secluded alcove, a settee and vintage butterfly chair lend themselves to intimate gatherings with the precious kitties.

▲ With their baby kitties, Wendy and Monica lounge beneath an old Japanese lantern in a garden alcove.

▶ The Addisons have expanded their living space by creating their very own "secret garden."

Style Tips

For Wendy and Monica, shopping is sheer bliss! The two regularly explore their favorite haunts. For them, a treasure hunt can be anywhere from the dirtiest junk stores to the funkiest vintage-clothing stores and anywhere in between. The Addisons helpfully provided the following tips to help you find your treasures:

1 Find "cheap junk stores" and check them out regularly—you'll find the most "serendipitous" things there (at the best prices, too).

2 Always be on the lookout for the unexpected.

3 At flea markets, always look under the table—that's where all the treasures are.

4 Don't limit yourself by restoring items to their intended use.

Style Checklist

✔ Rely on open-weave, transparent furniture to create the illusion of light, airy space. Some Addison examples are: open-back bistro chairs, an iron daybed, the rolling kitchen island, and the vintage wire bust.

✔ Utilize candles and oil lamps for soft lighting whenever and wherever possible.

✔ Puddle sheer fabrics and display vintage clothing for subtle touches of romance. Some Addison touches are: the bed canopy, the tablecloth, and the Japanese silk robe.

✔ Create dramatic effects by using high spaces to hang things, such as the Addison's oil lamps, trails of ivy, and bed canopy.

✔ Make use of things others would leave behind, such as old papers, ribbons, fabric scraps, and coffee cans.

743

The Albers'
"Bungalow
Bliss" on a
lazy autumn
desert
afternoon.

CHAPTER SIX

Bungalow Bliss

THE ALBER FAMILY HOME

TEN-MONTH-OLD ANNA, four-year-old Trent, and twelve-year-old Taylor can make a pretty eventful anything, but the Alber family is a surprisingly well-organized clan. Between shuttling Taylor off to voice lessons or drama class, keeping an eye on Trent's mischievous boy stuff in the backyard, or Anna's calls for attention, Kristen and Dan still manage to find time to travel together on national and international buying trips and squeeze in a few more minutes to host friendly gatherings and movie nights for the family. Perhaps it's their ability to balance the home's management—Kristen managing the arrangement, Dan providing the muscle, both supervising the children's chores—or just this family's sense of cooperation. Either way they have created a vibrant, peaceful space.

THE SUN IS intense and hot here, creating long and lazy days, that encourage you to pour a glass of lemonade and daydream out on the porch. The sprawling landscape and bright sun make for a relaxing

**The Alber Family Portrait (from left):
Kristen, Anna, Taylor, Dan, and Trent.**

▲ The front door is one of the many treasures Dan's found for the house. Its first life was as the front door of a general store in Austin, Texas. A simple wood panel has been added to its original iron grate, offering a weathered, though warm, welcome.

▶ When the Albers moved in, the fireplace and trim were painted a dark grayish-blue. With fresh white paint accented by warm yellow walls, the space was vividly transformed. Kristen's love for flowers is evident, and the theme is consistent, cheerful, and cozy.

oasis. Located on an old street of an older neighborhood, beneath the shady solace of pecan trees, Dan and Kristen Alber have made a home.

While growing up, Kristen spent many summer vacations with her grandmother in Kansas. She loved the aging neighborhoods of "old, beat-up" homes and how they "just felt so grand." Consequently, Kristen developed a deep appreciation and fascination for "older things"; in fact, she says, "*I'm* an old soul." When she met and married Dan, her appreciation began to grow into a passion that would lead the couple to open a quaint home store in downtown Mesa, Arizona. Several years, three children, and a dog later, this energetic team has settled into a formerly "old, beat-up" home of their own, beautifully renovating it and creating the style we've termed *Bungalow Bliss*.

BUNGALOW BLISS IS cottage, comfortable, and colorful. It's the dreamy and romantic feeling stirred by delicate trimmings of florals and icing layers of warm pastels. Although it is not perfection or all too flashy, it is not average or common at all. It is the confidence of an unexpected predictability and practical function. It is the careful follow-through of unassuming themes where rooms employ a specific personality and take on the unique eccentricity of a world all their own. It is peaceful, subtle, and altogether beautiful.

Relying heavily on the yard for increased space and comfort, Kristen and Dan spend the majority of their at-home time outside. They even lowered the porch railings so they could keep an eye on the kids while they play.

Inside, slipcovers and dark fabrics make for easy cleanup and low maintenance, although Kristen confesses, "It seems like we are always cleaning." In any event, the

▲ **No need to buy vases when you can use your glassware—especially if it's as beautiful as Kristen's vintage depression glass.**

◄ **Kristen is quick to remind us that the white dining table and chairs are full of nicks and scratches from constant, loving use. "They just add charm and character," she says.**

clean spaces and bright colors work together, as does the family itself, to compose a sweet place that is blissful.

THE FRONT PORCH is truly the first room of this home. With its welcoming swing and wicker rocker teamed with soft pillows and pots brimming with colorful flowers, the Alber's front porch is a wonderful way to enter the home. But what lies beyond, through the antique front door from a general store in Austin, Texas, intrigues us as we enter the living room. The room is bright and cheery, with vibrant yellow walls that playfully bounce the light that streams in through the wavy glass windows. Verging on a veneration of flowers, floral prints are everywhere. They're classic and beautiful but, most importantly, functional. After three small children and a white sofa and chairs, Kristen realized that the ability to hide a little dirt was extremely valuable. Beyond the fabric prints, flowers adorn lampshades, picture frames, rugs, and vintage still lifes. Combined with the soothing wall color, active light, and oversized seating the room has life. "It just makes me smile," says Kristen.

REFLECTING THE LIVELY feeling and warm sentiment of the living room, the dining room repeats the cheeriness but with a romantically vintage twist. Beneath the soft light of the porcelain yellow and white-rose chandelier from the 1930s, a whitewashed reproduction antique table and chairs center the space. Although it is white, a weathered finish allows for the Alber kids' wear and tear to go unnoticed. By combining a variety of different antique and vintage china, glassware, and silver, the table settings avert any possibility of rigid formality. In general, mixing and matching creates a more relaxed environment.

PREVIOUSLY CONSISTING OF just a counter and sink, the home's original kitchen was, in a word, horrible. It was not at all functional for the Albers, and desperately needed to be changed. Two years ago, armed with a sledgehammer, Dan gladly took to gutting the space and began the transformation. The finished product meets their daily family needs in both a practical and visually appealing way. In spite of its small size, the room has ample prep space and storage solutions, thanks to the oversized butcher block/counter top/center island. Pistachio walls and white cabinetry increase the space and disburse the light that comes from two small windows framing the sink. In order to complete the windows but maintain an optimum allowance for light, two valances have been fashioned from oval placemats that offer a punch of contrast.

▲ The Albers personalize their kitchen by displaying everything from collections of utensils, heirloom dishes, and cookbooks to scales or even personal memos. A bulletin board is a modern-day classic, serving to neatly collect photos, reminders, or whatever, keeping family members updated and in touch.

◄ Kristen enjoys cooking in the kitchen now that the remodeling has given her the needed storage space solutions.

▶ Someone's baking—or at least trying to. The kitchen island creates a great family workspace. (If baby Anna has her way, the marshmallows will be gone before the treats are finished!)

AT THE CENTER of the house, the family room is a space of durable comfort. Since it is a corridor between the living area and bedrooms, the room is a transitional space. Cushy red floor pillows and an overstuffed black sofa make an inviting spot for movies, TV, or games. While at first the dark colors might seem in conflict with the rest of the house, the unexpected contrast complements the house's overall softness. At the far end of the room lies a pleasant surprise—two antique corbels create an archway, a "custom look" that "reminds you of somewhere else," Kristen says, "and beckons you onward." Since the home previously afforded no indoor laundry space, another surprise hides in the room's corner cabinetry. Behind the doors of the unit, a washer and dryer have been cleverly disguised, increasing the room's utility.

▲ **Architectural surprises—two antique cornices—transition the family room to the hallway and beyond. According to Kristen, "Including pieces of the past really helps customize the house."**

◄ **The Albers utilized this hallway-like space by creating a family/transition room, relying on dark furnishings for durable use.** *(inset)* **Don't feel you have to hide your TV or other electronics. Placed atop a great piece like this black dresser, the space remains attractive and functional.**

► **Instead of hiding in an obscure corner or outside in the garage, this disguised washer and dryer saves space and allows for easy access in this specially built cabinet in the family room.**

THE MASTER BEDROOM is smooth, silky, and lustrous. A compromise was reached in the room's color, and they opted for a silvery blue instead of Kristen's preferred pastel palette. Cool, almost shiny bedding, mixed with just a few floral pillows, sumptuously dresses the bed beneath an antique crystal chandelier, an exquisite piece of their collection. But the room's statement piece is definitely the nearly nine-foot-tall whitewashed antique hutch. Dan rescued the piece while visiting the South and brought it home, giving it new purpose—an entertainment unit above with a dresser below.

▲ **Old painted barn wood with antique glass knobs makes a great peg rack, ideal for hanging everything from bags and belts, to even a basket of lavender.**

◄ **The romance of the master bedroom is unmistakable; the silvery-blue walls and bedding are a sleek twist that offer a contrasting compromise Dan can live with—it's not too feminine but fabulously chic.** *(inset)* **A massive, nearly nine-foot hutch fills an empty wall and hides a TV above and clothing below, increasing the closet space of this room.**

► **The narrow ledge of the hutch becomes a perfect spot for a pile of books and a collection of silver vases with some of Kristen's favorite blooms—calla lilies.**

CONTINUING THE CLASSIC feel of the bedroom, the master bath is simply elegant. Multiple and distinctly separate pieces have been combined to create a dramatic statement. On one side, the combination of three separate items—an antique mirror, an antique marble-top sink, and an antique crystal chandelier—are brought together to produce a dazzling display. At the other end, a contemporary version of the perhaps-expected claw-foot tub rests beneath yet another delicate chandelier.

▲ The oversized mirror atop the French marble sink reflects the delicately tiered crystal chandelier and creates a dramatic effect that is opulent yet practical. The mirror-less medicine cabinet provides useful shelving.

◄ The master bathtub provides a favorite respite, the faded floral valance and crystal chandelier above add a hint of color and soft light.

Taylor's room is tailor-made, right down to her favorite color, lavender, everywhere! This space can grow with her because it doesn't feel too young or too old.

▼ (inset bottom) The delicate collection of old miniature dolls is gently nestled on the hutch for easy accessibility and play.

▶ (inset top) The faded pink hutch is a quiet contrast to the lavender. Full of books, games, and a stereo, it's her very own entertainment unit.

▲ Trent's room features a transportation theme with a special emphasis on planes, thanks to his grandpa, who's taken a personal interest in passing on one of his passions.

(below right) **A Tweedle Dee and Tweedle Dum bird feeder may not appear to match the theme, but it is an undeniably fun addition to Trent's dresser top, which features two of his favorite characters from one of his favorite movies.**

▼ Everything here is kid-proof and hands-on. An old beat-up hutch stores books above with more toys below. The bench becomes a spot to curl up and read a book with dad or cozy up with a cuddly bear.

THE CHILDREN each have distinct rooms that share the common tie of a personality-reflective theme. Taylor's room is exactly what she wanted—soft, sweet, and girly. Lavender-washed walls, a patchwork quilt atop a French-style bed, and crystal-beaded accessories all recall a young girl's dreams of fantasy. Another oversized antique hutch stands guard in the corner, lending its pale pink hue to the gentle quality of Taylor's space.

On the other hand (and down the hall), Trent's room is fittingly all boy. Full of building blocks, trucks, trains, and airplanes, the space is lively and active. The little-boy, tough blue-striped bedding is the perfect choice paired with the red high-back bench and the antique pine hutch. Everything in the room is sturdy and hands-on. Trent is free to touch, tackle, and tumble on anything in his space—which is just the way every child's room should be. The pine hutch also serves as a great display board for his latest artwork, which can be taped directly on and easily removed.

◀◀ The chalkboard serves as a learning tool for Trent to practice his **ABCs** and also get loving reminders from Mom. Just above, the old-fashioned-looking school clock is appropriately placed. On the side of the pine hutch, Trent's fashioned his own bulletin board, taping his weekly masterpieces for all to enjoy.

◀ A sweet collection is gathered on the wall, including Kristen's own "Miss America" swimsuit from her childhood—appropriately given, as she is the daughter of Miss America 1966.

▲ "ANNA," topped in pretty pink gingham, floats above a faded floral chair and flower-topped table—a whimsical alternative to other more expected wall hangings.

◀ The nursery is delicate and darling. Somehow you expect to hear lullabies playing in the background to complete the precious experience this space provides.

FINALLY, BABY ANNA has a delicately precious place all her own. Bathed in shades of pink, the nursery is enchanting. A reproduction iron crib is laced with faded floral linens and accompanied by an impressive mirrored wardrobe and cozy armchair. All the warm pastels are highlighted by yet another dainty antique crystal chandelier. Heirloom baby dresses hang on the walls and are accompanied by vintage teacups and small bouquets of fresh flowers.

◂ *(top)* **Pink patterns are mixed and matched in the heirloom iron crib fit for a princess.** *(middle)* **A vintage dress hangs from a hand-painted wooden hanger from a white coat rack, which is a practical piece that can be utilized throughout the changes of any child's room.**

▴ **Pretty in pink, Anna talks on her vintage phone.**

◂ **The kids' bathroom, painted mint green, is original down to its built-in medicine cabinet. A few simple adornments complete the space: vintage tin canisters hide tissue, a peg rack holds hand towels and Taylor's necklaces. All of this is crowned with a hand-painted hanging glass lamp.**

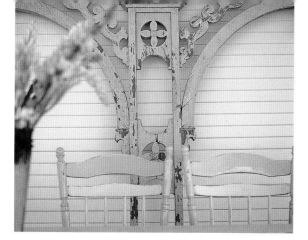

▲ This architectural element, with its handcrafted appeal and intricate detail, easily leans against a wall, as an eye-catching conversation piece and stunning statement.

◄ An old-fashioned wraparound porch full of vintage furniture, architectural elements, and patchwork pillows is a soothing refuge.

► The Albers' yard is designed with plenty of space for Taylor to easily pull Trent in the wagon until Ben tries to hitch a ride.

▼ The perfect backyard accoutrement—a pint-sized mini-bungalow for the pint-sized Albers.

THE MAIN FOCUS of the yard is the home's grand wraparound porch. Kristen and Dan utilize this space a great deal and have extended their living area by filling the porch with other functional and beautiful pieces of their collection. A whitewashed table is joined by a group of antique chairs and a pretty bench, which has been fitted with a well-worn skirt and plush pillows. Backdropped by a fabulous salvaged architectural piece, and a large, comfy, vintage wicker sofa, the area has become a family "room" in itself. And just beyond the porch's low railing, the rest of the yard opens into a sprawling lawn and play space where the kids and Ben, the dog, rove. Tucked into a close corner, Dan has constructed a playhouse (vaguely reminiscent of the house) for the rambunctious threesome. Although beautiful, the area's true value lies in its functionality. It is indeed just another room "in" (or should we say "out" of) the house.

◄ Simply tossed about, flea market finds
make fun and interesting groupings.

▼ This chandelier is from the Albers'
exquisite collection.

Style Tips

Kristen and Dan are perpetually on the lookout for great additions. Kristen realizes that she has a good eye, but says that it's not hard for anyone to find great things. The Albers gave the following shopping advice:

1 Don't get caught up with matching.

2 Go with your heart—get what you love.

3 Look for things that reflect who you are.

4 Don't start what you can't finish—if you buy a project, make sure you have the time and resources to work on it.

Style Checklist

☑ Layer cheerful pastel colors in walls and trim, floors and rugs, upholstery and accents.

☑ Use distressed, painted furniture as opposed to natural woods.

☑ Collect old light fixtures to replace new ones.

☑ When in doubt, use flowers—vases of them, pictures of them, fabric, too.

☑ Remember, antiques are not always necessary—reproductions work just as well and may often be sturdier and cost-effective.

The brick path lined in
creeping vines and the old
postman's mailbox outside
the garden gate intrigue and
welcome visitors and
passersby.

CHAPTER SEVEN

Euro Nouveau

THE TANOV-EMERSON FAMILY HOME

GATHERINGS DURING THE SUMMERTIME are frequent occurrences at the Tanov-Emerson home of Isabelle, Erica, Steve, and Hugo. In fact, "we are in the backyard pretty much all summer," notes Erica. When they are not entertaining in it, Erica and one-year-old Hugo even devote their few free moments to therapeutically tending it. However, a bit more adventurous, Isabelle (seven years old) and Steve prefer getting away from it all on the ski slopes or at the family's cabin in the snow. Yet, the weekly violin lessons (Isabelle), trips to the flea market (Erica), and music making (Steve) usually consume most of their time, and the family rarely gets around to enjoying either of their favorite activities very often. The spare seconds of the week are usually spent at the park, with grandma at the Ice Capades, or by the fire as Steve and Isabelle present selections from their latest musical repertoire. That's the feeling of this home. It's the kind of fireside peace that's found in the comfort of an old, timeworn chair. Erica and Steve commented, "It's so casual that nothing is off limits, every room is [the

The Tanov-Emerson Family Portrait (from left): Isabelle, Erica, Steve, and Hugo.

◄ **A backless frame becomes an element of design while a tiny framed picture hangs from a thin piece of ribbon, becoming somehow larger and more important.**

(below left) **Fresh flowers are a must in this family house. Just a single bloom breathes life into this darkened corner.**

▼ **The carefree simplicity is what defines this family's style. The perfect example—the coatrack, vintage umbrella perched above, whitewashed slender chair below. The effect is effortless style.**

children's] to enjoy and live in. It all works well . . . slips can be washed and surfaces scuffed . . . we'll never have a super formal house." With general chores delegated, and admittedly a little outside help, things just flow. The only real challenges the young couple faced was in lighting what were originally very dark rooms and finding enough storage/closet space. Not to worry, with the aide of bright walls and lighter furnishings, the home has been totally transformed and, thanks to Steve's organizational skills, they've made room for storage (like the "dresser" in the dining room for Hugo's clothes). Closet space or not, the home is absolutely amazing and delightfully charming.

Tucked away down one of the innumerable and secluded neighborhood streets of Berkeley, California, Erica and Steve have fashioned an inspirational, serene home. Inauspicious and humble, their bungalow peeks out from behind an aged picket fence and a cozy overgrowth of antique rose bushes. Ah, bella!

Both were born and raised in the Bay Area, yet ironically the two didn't meet until they were on the other side of the country. While following their dreams in New York City—Steve, an aspiring musician, and Erica, a fashion designer to be—the two fell in love and soon married. However, opting for the more familiar pace, Erica and Steve moved back to the Bay Area to settle and begin a family. With the birth of their first child, Isabelle, the couple sought a more comfortable space to call home. Finally, in 1997, Erica, Steve, and Isabelle moved into their 1918 Craftsman-style bungalow and inadvertently began what has evolved into their own personal signature style—a little something we like to call *Euro Nouveau*.

EURO NOUVEAU IS A FREE-SPIRITED, pure, effortless notion. It evokes feelings of calm and ideals of respite. It's the natural beauty intrinsic in the combination of timeless and elegant objects with new but classic materials. In Erica's words, it's "comfortable, relaxed, nothing has a set place." Erica's insatiable desire to collect is balanced by Steve's need for minimalist surroundings, resulting in a style all their own, with consistent themes of neutral backdrops, vintage finds, and fresh flowers.

BECAUSE SHE IS A COLLECTOR by nature and designer by trade, Erica has gathered an incredible assortment of textiles, garments, and clothing. When we first walked through the front door, we were drawn to a simple coatrack draped with the family's coats, scarves, and umbrellas. It was fabulous—simple and, best of all, functional! Who would have thought that something so ordinary and necessary for everyday living could look so good? To the right of the coatrack, Erica and Steve transformed a preexisting closet, of original, nine-foot-tall, shuttered doors into a family entertainment unit housing everything from the stereo and CDs to craft supplies.

▲ Isabelle and Dad relaxing in the comfortable living room.

◄ The living room serves as a playroom for the kids, a TV room, and a formal entertainment space. *(inset bottom)* The original fireplace, a patchwork of mismatched bricks, creates a warm focal point for the space. Erica's simple accessory additions keep the feeling light, natural, and easy. *(inset top)* Erica collects old jars and bottles for good reason. This beautifully labeled apothecary is stunning on its own but even better and more interesting when topped with merely a few stems of white hydrangea.

▼ A glossy white armoire is gently adorned with a filigree-framed picture of the Madonna, and on its side, Erica creatively hangs pictures of the kids. The blatant imperfection is key.

(below right) Hugo can comfortably spend time at his play table (sometimes referred to as the coffee table) without mom worrying about nicks and scratches. After all, they just add character.

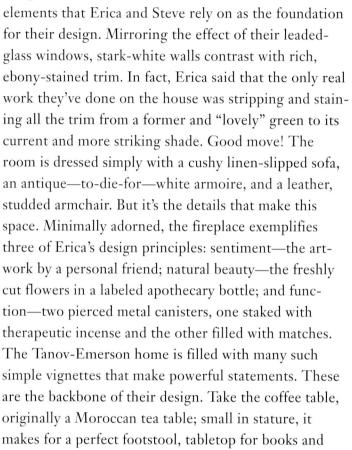

TO THE LEFT OF THE FRONT door and opposite the entertainment closet beckons the family room. The first things we notice about this room are the architectural elements that Erica and Steve rely on as the foundation for their design. Mirroring the effect of their leaded-glass windows, stark-white walls contrast with rich, ebony-stained trim. In fact, Erica said that the only real work they've done on the house was stripping and staining all the trim from a former and "lovely" green to its current and more striking shade. Good move! The room is dressed simply with a cushy linen-slipped sofa, an antique—to-die-for—white armoire, and a leather, studded armchair. But it's the details that make this space. Minimally adorned, the fireplace exemplifies three of Erica's design principles: sentiment—the artwork by a personal friend; natural beauty—the freshly cut flowers in a labeled apothecary bottle; and function—two pierced metal canisters, one staked with therapeutic incense and the other filled with matches. The Tanov-Emerson home is filled with many such simple vignettes that make powerful statements. These are the backbone of their design. Take the coffee table, originally a Moroccan tea table; small in stature, it makes for a perfect footstool, tabletop for books and beverages, or a play surface for Hugo.

BEYOND THE FAMILY ROOM we enter the dining room. Again architectural facets form the backdrop of the room's design. A built-in hutch filled with a myriad of creamy white dishes and antique glassware anchors the dining table and provides a focal point. The antique dark-wood table combines timeless beauty with its classic design and necessary function by doubling as a desktop for Erica when she works from home. By the way, the built-in hutch drawers hide their office paper-work—talk about multipurposed furnishings!

◄ The dining room is painted in a robin's-egg blue, gently contrasting the ebony-stained trim. A stick of bamboo becomes a curtain rod, and an antique lace runner from Erica's incredible linen collection adds romance and texture.

► A pewter pitcher finds new purpose as a vase and, joined with a pair of candlesticks and antique salt and pepper shakers, makes a delightful centerpiece.

AS WE MADE OUR WAY INTO the kitchen we were intrigued by the combination of surfaces: the slate green Corian countertop, the butcher-block island, and the stainless steel stove. Individual and distinctive on their own, these large surfaces together create a unique kitchen experience. The oversized island serves as a chopping block for food preparation as well as an impromptu dining table. The two hand-blown glass fixtures above, a wedding gift from a friend, add a contemporary crown to the room. Just beside the stove, Erica and Steve have opted for a nontraditional design to the hanging pot rack. Instead they've layered multiple wall racks from floor to ceiling. What a great idea and an incredible statement too! And the pantry, unlike most, stands exposed and open, offering its wares for easy access. We were personally inspired by Erica's silverware—her collection consists of not one single matching set but of many coordinated mismatched sets. The concept of not matching but coordinating is at the heart of this room—more importantly, this home's design.

▲ *(top)* **An open pantry is layered with dishes, pitchers, and glassware as an opposing wall becomes a sort of scrap or bulletin board covered in family pictures and meaningful cards.** *(top right)* **A salt-canister-turned-planter below another vintage Madonna is somehow magical and serene.** *(above right)* **At the end of the counter, a beautiful black cabinet stands beside a message board (frequently adorned with Isabelle's artwork), combining timeless beauty with practical art.** *(above left)* **A collection of hanging knives is a great way to save counter space.**

▶ **The long narrow wall beside the oven is cleverly covered in a vertical tower of hanging pot racks, which is smart looking and practical at the oven's side.**

◀ **The butcher-block countertop hosts a mismatched group of leather-topped bar stools that create an interesting appeal.** *(inset top)* **Another corner of the kitchen feels entirely different with slate-green countertops, yet the variation is somehow harmonious and tranquil.**
(inset bottom) **Leaving the cooking spices out in assorted jars and canisters is not only practical but practically adorable.**

THE PEACEFUL WHIMSY OF SEVEN-YEAR-OLD Isabelle's room most adequately captures the soulful simplicity of the home's personal style. Tranquil cream walls and furnishings along with faded floral bed linens are accented with vintage toys and undressed windows, making for a soft, soothing little girl's dream room. No primary colors here! A cluster of cubicles work to organize Isabelle's tiny treasures, and though the room afforded no closet space, an antique dresser and armoire provide the solution to this storage problem. Above the antique French bed, a collection of sentimental toys sitting atop an old wire shelf is framed by Isabelle's own artwork. On the floor, a collection of Isabelle's shoes lies stashed beneath the dresser, and in the window, a collection of bells hangs from an old wooden coat hanger, warding off the bogeyman.

▲ **A life-size painting found in a New York flea market gives a punch of color beside the whitewashed dresser.** *(top right)* **Hanging in the window, a wind chime Dad made helps to keep Isabelle protected from the bogeyman.**

◄ **Isabelle's room is a little girl's dream, combining timeless pieces of the past with cleverly stored objects for play. The pint-size cubicles keep toys and books organized while offering hands-on access.**

► **Isabelle and Hugo respond playfully to the casual atmosphere of the room.**

▼ **Isabelle's shoes peek out from under the dresser.**

The fresh white bathroom has vintage appeal. Its original mirrored cabinet hides daily essentials.

COOL AND CALM, THE bathroom is simple yet functional. The consistency of tone-on-tone makes for a relaxing haven. The fact that this room is so stark, so simple, somehow makes this space stunning despite its characteristically small size. Original architectural elements make up for an abundance of bathroom fixtures and help keep the space precise and tidy, as Steve wishes.

THE MASTER BEDROOM IS, in a word (or two), romantically sleek. No headboard, no footboard, no frills. Erica and Steve remain consistent in choosing the sentimentally essential details—the artwork above the bed, the heirloom baby shoes on the nightstand trimmed by the antique jewelry, the layers of vintage linens—all whisper stories of times past. This is part of Erica and Steve's passion, to find timeless remnants "you can love in your lifetime that have been loved many lifetimes before and will be loved for lifetimes to come." Nestled in the corner and tucked with cozy, soft bedding is baby Hugo's crib—another solution to a common design dilemma—what happens when the baby comes before the nursery? While Erica and Steve await the new addition to their home, Hugo's own heirlooms-to-be have already begun. On a pint-size antique painted chair, a small box bearing Hugo's name holds the beginnings of his shoe collection, and above, an antique peg rack displays memoirs of precious moments past.

▲ *(top)* **The blush pink lampshade mirrors the freshly picked roses, which provide the room's only color.**

(top right and above) **Floating Japanese paper lanterns create a mobile for baby Hugo and complement a nearby watercolor.**

◄ **The master bedroom echoes the family's effortless elegance, which includes elements that are romantically sleek.**

▶ **Hugo's space, shared with Mom and Dad, holds his clothes and shoe collection.**

OVERGROWN AND SECLUDED, the family's garden is a self-described "sanctuary in the city." Erica has an obsession for roses! Wild, climbing the fences, creeping along the ground and up the walls, they provide a secret garden all their own. According to Steve, the best thing about an overgrown yard is that you don't have to be on top of it. For Erica, the fringe benefits are fresh flowers inside year-round.

▲ The back patio extends beyond the kitchen, complete with a potted herb garden and outdoor dining, as the family loves to entertain.

◄ Even in the middle of autumn, this family enjoys their backyard with its cozy seating areas amidst flagstone pathways and surrounded in the overgrowth of vintage rosebushes and vines.

► There is even a space for Isabelle to swing!

▲ Steve's workspace doubles
  as a guesthouse in the
  separate cottage out back.
  More cubicles store his
  album collection and
  vintage books.

  (above right) **A
  noteworthy, French
  painted mirror hangs
  unexpectedly above the
  kitchen counter.**

▶ Out for their morning
  walk, led by Buster.

Style Tips

As with many artistic collectors, Erica and Steve love shopping the flea markets and local antiques shops, and though Erica does not consider herself much of a shopper, when asked for some tips, she and Steve came up with the following:

1 Go for quality rather than quantity.

2 Pick pieces for life, not current fads or trends.

3 What you don't see, you won't miss.

4 If you like it, get it!

Style Checklist

✔ Maintain a neutral furniture palette: cream sofa, dark wood tones in tables and chairs, statement white pieces like beds, armoires, etc.

✔ Utilize versatile vintage accents. Some Tanov-Emerson examples are: the Moroccan tea table that acts as a coffee table and play surface, the apothecary jars and pitchers that become vases, and backless frames that act as design elements.

✔ Incorporate sentimental artwork, paying little attention to scale.

✔ Display antique and vintage textiles everywhere—on tables, beds, windows, etc.

✔ Refrain from clutter—allow effortless and subtle statements to stand alone.

The older home has been updated with a new coat of paint (dark taupe), and the walkway by removing the preexisting (as Dirk says, "ugly!") pathway and replacing it with simple cement stepping stones, poured by Dirk. Leaving space in between for grass, and lining both sides with mostly lavender, the entry feels refreshed.

Contemporary Country

THE WANLASS FAMILY HOME

WHETHER SHUFFLING THE KIDS to extracurricular activities, hosting friends at an afternoon brunch, planting the garden beds, or escaping on weekend getaways to the museums, mountains, or anything in between, this family of six (plus two dogs, one snake, and eight chickens) is always on the move. Tirzah acknowledges with a cool smile, "We're nutty—always heading in a million different directions at once—like every other family, I'm sure—but that's why, for us, our home has to be calming and peaceful, to bring us back down to Earth." The pale muted tones, the neutral slipcovers, the soft layers of texture accented with subtle drops of color on faded prints are all a testament to that notion. This is a home you walk into and feel instant serenity, comfort, and coziness—it's homey! And just then, all the kids come running down the stairs—Lucas, of course, sliding down the banister— and you remember just how homey it really is. "Child-proof? What's that?" Dirk laughs. The young parents both admit their style has always been what it is. As a result, it's what the kids were raised in and is all

The Wanlass Family Portrait (from left): Lacey Ellen, Lucas, Tirzah holding "Baby Sam," Locksley Hannah, Dirk, Shane, and Henry in the front.

▲ The tree-lined streets provide a shadowy haven for football with Dad and daily inspiration for early morning jogs and evening walks.

(above right) Down the hallway, a simple peg rail holds a straw bag with a couple of sentimental hats.

▶ Smart storage solutions make the main entry a clutter-free thoroughfare. The iron coatrack collects jackets, handbags, etc.; the bag below holds shoes and umbrellas; the pine washstand offers surface area for keys and coins; and the stacked baskets hold toys and the kid's sports equipment.

▼ Every home needs this—a huge money bowl by the front door that collects loose change, keys, sunglasses, wallets (and whatever else that seems to get scattered about the house) in one safe and convenient place.

they know. Yes, there are breakables, but nothing has a value so high it can't be replaced, especially since Tirzah loves the challenge of finding fun and outrageously affordable items for their home. And the white furnishings and bed linens against the neutral backdrops are actually preferred by this family to help keep them "on top" of cleaning. When it's dirty, they know it instantly, and with a quick toss in the laundry, the house remains fresh and tidy. Other than meeting the test of fitting all their furnishings into a house half the size of their previous one, this family is so content with their space, both indoors and out, that an obvious sense of what's meant to be fills this home and clearly meets their needs of style and function.

THE TREES HUNCH over their street, like massive and protective guardians standing watch. They are imposing yet welcoming. They hug the rows of homes tucked neatly beneath their boughs. And in the very middle of them all, Dirk and Tirzah and Lacey and Shane and . . . (all the rest of them!) have settled into a perfectly charming and cozy space.

Married at just twenty-one (Dirk) and nineteen (Tirzah), the California natives set out with the same struggles common to every young couple. Rent and other bills were primary to luxuries like a pretty house. However, resolute and energetic Tirzah was determined to turn even their first place (a 500-square-foot apartment, formerly a lumberman's garage) into a dream that even caught the eye of several national publications! Nearly thirteen years and four children later, the two just recently purchased a 1930s bungalow on a sleepy and peaceful street in Vallejo, California. Although it is not new or custom-built and required a lot of elbow grease just to move in, the old charm that only a "mature" home offers was what first attracted them. And combined with Tirzah's phenomenal savvy for smart buying and clever space solutions and Dirk's knowledgeable sense for custom building, the young couple has beautifully composed a space we fittingly call *Contemporary Country*.

If design were a scale designated by concepts like modern, eclectic, and traditional, somewhere in the middle lies *Contemporary Country*. It blends an appreciation for the old and an admiration of what's new. It combines the cozy warmth and casual homeness of country with the contrast of the sleek urban modernity of contemporary. While founded in the classic concepts basic to country, the contemporary twist allows perpetual evolution, creating an avenue for an eclectic mix of the best of both worlds. This is what Tirzah loves the most, how her home is a "canvas" for her to paint masterpieces over and over and over again, as the mood and season strikes.

THROUGH THE FRONT DOOR and immediately into the living room, a first impression is definitely made by the scale of space—this home is small! Not even a distinct foyer . . . space is clearly at a premium. But rest assured, this issue is addressed with other smart storage solutions. At the base of the stairs, a reproduction iron coat rack clutches the family's coats, bags, and even a few hats. Simply stacked, worn wicker trunks hold books, toys, and sports equipment, while a small, antique English pine washstand allows for cabinet space as well as a surface for keys and spare change. An entry hall has been created from the living room's corners.

THE CONTEMPORARY BONES of the living room are accented with antique trimmings. The sharp lines of the sofa against the scalloped cutwork of the Venetian glass mirror and the hand-carved rustic Moroccan table work together to create a mood of subtle chic. Combining all these different styles works! This is a home full of textures: wicker, leather, linen, bamboo, antique pine, iron, and silk. Though based on the subdued neutral palette of the large staple pieces (sofas, armoires, chairs), muted colors found in the pale blue walls, antique green piano, multicolored and timeworn pillows, and fresh flowers also flourish. The idea of broadly mixing varied elements is fundamental to the Wanlasses' design plan. However, mindful of the concern for space, Tirzah recognized the requirement for a "cautious" mix. While colors and textures are combined, it is important to begin with a fresh canvas. By repainting the oak banister, mantel, kickboards, and trim white, a noncompetitive environment was established, affording an easily transitional backdrop.

▲ *(top)* **From another view of the living room we see how two different glass-front pine cabinets have been combined to make one beautiful bookcase with room for a stereo, while an affordable great space-saver sits at the end of the coffee table—a canvas slipcovered folding chair.** *(above left)* **Locksley and Luke doing some of what kids do best.** *(above right)* **On the mantel, a series of bottles holds curly willow branches and fresh red dahlias beside a mini-collection of old clocks (another one of Tirzah's favorite flea-market finds).**

◄ **The living room is a soft palette of timeworn neutrals. The ice blue walls and the carved, green Indonesian coffee table add just enough color to bring life and subtle drama.**

▶ **Dirk sits with Luke and Henry for a quick story.**

AS IT IS FOR MOST MODERN families, the need for relaxing downtime space is more essential than the need to have formal rooms. What to do? Answer: Turn the unutilized space, whatever it is, into a gathering room. Tirzah and Dirk are not formal entertainers. They much prefer the intimate coziness of a kitchen table to a traditional and formal dining room. So they took their formal dining room and turned it into an official "hangout" spot. Another sofa, some comfy chairs and a television define the room. The television is not hidden behind the closed doors of a cabinet but rather perched atop an antique pine dresser. A cushy couch is slipcovered in a darker, still neutral fabric, great for the wear and tear four kids and two dogs create, while the pine writing desk—artfully topped with some of Tirzah's flea-market finds and antique ledgers—doubles as video storage space.

▲ Tirzah's love for the warmth of texture, the shine of metal, and the softness of flowers was the inspiration that created this intimate space.

◀ Peeking into the formal dining room turned family room, we see how an old Chinese candle lantern has been converted easily into a hanging fixture. And a nineteenth century upright piano (yes, it's green!) finishes off the living room on its own wall, covered in piles of books and old sheet music.

▶ A magnifying glass sitting on old ledgers beckons everyone to look closely (everything is hands-on in this family room).

▼ A vintage white oval platter loaded with shells from family trips to the beach makes another sentimental statement. *(bottom right)* Old leather-bound ledgers sit atop an antique pine mapmaker's desk; a vintage still life beside a rusted wall sconce makes an asymmetrical but balanced grouping.

The Wanlasses fell in love with their home's original kitchen, especially the black-and-yellow-tiled counters. After removing the doors to apply a fresh coat of white paint (that Tirzah swears will transform any outdated kitchen), they decided to keep them off, allowing the stacks of monochromatic dishes, pitchers, and glassware to make an almost industrial statement. *(below left)* The other side of the kitchen—Old World meets New World with the stainless-steel fridge, and a tiered bamboo cart with chopping block above and stacked pots and pans below. European carving boards lean above the stove and clever containers hold onions, potatoes, and utensils for storage and easy access. *(below right)* Originally meant for the phone, now home to a delicate orchid, this niche has been surrounded with a collage of watercolors and still lifes.

▶ *(top)* The casual dining space comfortably seats the Wanlass family, with its assortment of wicker chairs, slipped chairs, and oversized paint-chipped bench. *(bottom left)* An old store scale weighs in on form and function, doubling as a "fruit basket" when not in use. *(bottom right)* Fresh fruit is both displayed and made easily available to the kids.

QUITE OFTEN TODAY, people seek to create their own customized kitchen—and that's good! Custom cabinets and other modern appliances allow for optimal functionality, solving problems that have plagued us in the past. Older kitchens commonly lack storage, counter space, and many other conveniences; however, there is something to be said for choosing to confront those difficulties head-on. The Wanlasses chose to embrace their seventy-year-old kitchen, right down to its original black-and-yellow tile countertops! In response to its challenge for storage, Tirzah has incorporated other non-kitchen pieces. An antique pie safe houses cookbooks, extra glassware, and other odds and ends. A bamboo-and-rattan butler cart supports pots and pans, utensils, and a chopping block conveniently at the oven's side. And closed doors have been removed from the two hanging cupboards over the counter, allowing for easy accessibility while keeping clutter to a minimum.

Since this is a three-bedroom home, the children share rooms. While the boys' room overflows with toys, maps, trophies, and boy stuff, the girls share a more open and delicate feminine area.

▲ **A great alternative to poster-clad walls— an easy-to-make magnet board. It's a simple piece of sheet metal with scalloped edges, cut by Dad.**

◄ **Lacey and Locksley sleep in their very own Theatre of Dreams. A simple diamond motif was created on the floor by measuring and outlining the pattern, then filling it in with white wood stain. (inset) Lacey's vintage desk acts as a work space for homework and a vanity space for grooming.**

► **Lacey, who dreams of becoming a fashion designer, has created her very own masterpiece to personalize her space. On a piece of canvas from the local craft store, she's painted her "dream wedding dress," making a sweet, sentimental statement in the room.**

LACEY (TWELVE) AND Locksley (six)—share a large room that adequately addresses the diverse needs of both girls. Realizing the importance of light in the room, Tirzah made simply draped sheer panels for the windows from a vintage Indian sari. The pale lavender walls allow the light to bounce, making the space even bigger. The bed, dressed in layers of whites, hides Locksley's trundle (not photographed) while other white furnishings hide clothing, toys, and more girl stuff. Locksley has ample floor space for dolls and toys while Lacey's whitewashed desk doubles as a beauty station and surface for her homework and laptop. And a clever solution to the timeless question of what to do with those not-so-pretty teen-idol posters—a stylish magnet board. Fashioned from a single piece of sheet metal and finished with scalloped edges (snipped by Dad), the board collects the posters and pictures neatly in one spot and provides more space for the girls to creatively display their passions.

▲ A grouping of boy stuff is created with jars of marbles, game balls, vintage paints, airplanes, flags, and a retro lava lamp.

◄ The bedroom features antique pine youth beds that the boys can enjoy for years. The look is frequently changed by layering different blankets, quilts, or pillows. *(inset)* The boys keep organized with a chrome utility shelf that supports games, TV, and videos, old toys, and Snaky, the pet boa.

► An old fish painting is crested with vintage letters "S & L," which of course stand for Shane and Lucas.

▼ The timeless accessory for every boy's room—the classic ship in a bottle.

SHANE (ELEVEN) AND LUCAS (seven) are as inquisitive and rambunctious as most boys their age. Consequently, their room is brimming with treasures, discoveries, and memorabilia from their own and from other's adventures. Two twin antique pine beds fitted with neutral bedding and reproduction Civil War blankets are topped with an assortment of plaid, striped, and vintage souvenir pillows. A chrome utility shelf designates the center of the room—an entertainment center, display case, and home to Shane's pet boa, Snaky. What's fun about this particular room is that you can always add to it—it's never set. From the antique marbles and vintage bowling pins to the television and video games, all of its contents are completely functional as Shane and Lucas play with it all!

THE FAMILY BATH POSED the greatest challenge. This was the only room that had been remodeled (poorly) and so required a bit more work. By simply removing the former pressboard vanity and marble-like countertop, ample space was made available for two freestanding salvaged sinks. The walls whisper an ice blue hue, while antique stained glass, hung directly in front of the existing window, warms the light and enlarges the room. An inexpensive and creative alternative to a typical light fixture is made by wrapping a hanging socket with pliable twigs and bits of moss gathered from the yard. A pair of frameless, round, beveled mirrors completes the look.

▲ A "nature inspired" light fixture is created with twigs and moss.

◄ This is the only room the Wanlass Family has remodeled, removing the outdated oak cabinet with marble-looking sink top and replacing it with double wall-mounted porcelain sinks found at the local salvage yard. Shown here without sink skirts, the look is more urban/contemporary. With skirts (Tirzah often hangs burlap ones), the look is softened. The idea of having options is key. (inset) More of the family's vacation souvenirs have been appropriately placed in the bath.

▶ In the Wanlass home, one of the first things accomplished is the removal and replacement of the bathroom towel racks by peg rails or hooks to allow room for everyone's towel. Another great idea: Dirk's taken an old framed stained-glass window and hung it in front of the existing one, allowing in colorful light and, more importantly, providing complete privacy.

The master bedroom is white on white. *(inset)* At bedside, a warm grouping of old piled books, a horn bowl (for jewelry or change), and a single pewter candleholder with a green sap bucket of white dahlias call for dreams of nostalgic romance.

▲ Lacey, Locksley, and Sam enjoy the coziness of the stairway.

▶ (below right) The backyard is decked in a collage of furniture pieces, from the teak table and chairs to the wicker rockers and swing to the weathered Adirondack chairs overlooking the lawn. Tossed floral pillows add color and comfort. An old toolbox is given a new life as a flower trough full of trailing seasonal blooms.

▼ Out back, the kids have ample room to watch their baby chicks grow.

WHITE ON WHITE, the master bedroom, perches atop its own flight of stairs. Fortunately, the space already possessed architectural characteristics that truly set it off. The vaulted ceiling, planked walls, and a dormered alcove form almost a nest. The room totally wraps around you. Again, neutral bedding and plush pillows surrounded by antique pine and wicker increase a feeling of hominess. And candles and vintage flea market finds perpetuate a sense of old romance.

FOR A FAMILY OF SIX, the outside space is just as important as the inside. In the back a meandering brick patio surrounded by flowering bushes, low-hanging palms, and a sixty-foot redwood is the perfect set for extended family living. A teak table and chairs are shadowed by a freestanding market umbrella and overlook a spacious lawn where kids, dogs, and chickens roam. A pair of Adirondack chairs mixes well with a two-seater wicker rocker, vintage metal folding chairs, and painted benches. Tirzah says, "During the warm weather we live outside" and so this collection of textures, colors, and surfaces is a natural extension of their home.

▲ **A collection of pitchers and teapots lines a kitchen shelf beside hand-blown eggs from the family's chickens.**

Style Tips

Growing up in a family of eight, Tirzah learned the value of bargain shopping at a young age. While they're constantly on the hunt for exciting additions to their home, the Wanlasses limit their search to treasures that are a great deal. "It's actually a lot of fun. We go to flea markets and antique fairs as a family and search for treasures together. I also have my favorite local home stores I frequent regularly—they're good for inspiration." Here are some of the Wanlass family's shopping tips:

1 Buy things that are transitional, that can be moved from one space in your home to another.

2 Don't be afraid to bargain—but only at flea markets and antiques fairs.

3 Look for things that are multipurpose and durable. For example, we like antique pine because it's aged and weathered; if our kids scratch it, then character and charm are added.

4 Beauty is in the eye of the beholder; don't be swayed by naysayers. Go with your instinct.

5 Look for sales at local manufacturers; you can find some of the best "steals" ever!

Style Checklist

✔ Begin with neutral backdrops like white walls or pale hints of color.

✔ Layer things—upholstered pieces with pillows, chairs with throws, tables with books, windows with bamboo blinds and simple panels.

✔ Keep the furniture simple—use neutral solids and natural fibers for seating; choose antique pine for surfaces, storage, and tabletops.

✔ Accent with vintage (flea-market finds) and contemporary pieces (lamps and functional accessories).

✔ Combine collections. Some Wanlass Family examples are: a collage of still lifes, a dish of seashells, a grouping of vintage clocks, or a shelf of pitchers.

✔ Allow personalized themes to develop: old and new toys in the boys' room, vintage cooking accents in the kitchen, seashore treasures in the bath.

Resources

Testu Family Favorites

Interieur Perdu (French antiques)
340 Bryant Street
San Francisco, CA 94107
(415) 543-1616

Swallowtail (antiques/vintage finds)
2217 Polk Street
San Francisco, CA 94107
(415) 567-1555

Soularch Gallery (art)
4033A Judah Street
San Francisco, CA 94122
(415) 759-4100

Verdigris Gallery (ceramics)
The Cannery
2801 Leavenworth Street
San Francisco, CA 94133
(415) 446-2898

Zonal (home accents/furniture)
568 Hayes Street
San Francisco, CA 94102
(415) 255-9307

Adams Family Favorites

Acushnet River Antiques Mall
(antiques)
72 Killburn Street
New Bedford, MA 02740
(508) 992-8878

Chelsea Antiques (antiques)
148 Petaluma Boulevard North
Petaluma, CA 94952
(707) 763-7686

Janet's Antiques (antiques)
3800 University Avenue
Madison, WI 53705
(608) 238-3300

Livery Antiques (antiques)
303 Commerce Street
Mineral Point, WI
(608) 987-3833

New Bedford Antiques Mall
(antiques)
85 Coggeshall Street
New Bedford, MA 02746
(508) 993-9900

Summerhouse
(home accents/furniture)
21 Throckmorton Avenue
Mill Valley, CA 94941
(415) 383-6695

Burch Family Favorites

Jon Martens (architect)
5230 North 16th Street
Phoenix, AZ 85016
(602) 265-9800

Willows (home accents/furniture)
6137 North Scottsdale Road
Scottsdale, AZ 85250
(480) 348-9599

Oberoi Family Favorites

Lunares
(aluminum accents/furniture)
174 Valencia Street
San Francisco, CA 94103
(415) 621-0764
lunaressf@aol.com

Addison Family Favorites

Tancredi and Morgan
(antique linens)
7174 Carmel Valley Road
Carmel, CA 93923
(831) 625-4477

Theatre of Dreams
(original objects)
P.O. Box 20
Port Costa, CA 94569
(510) 787-2164

Alber Family Favorites

Domestic Bliss
(home accents/furniture)
140 West Maine Street
Mesa, AZ 85201
(480) 733-0552
www.Domesticblissdesign.com

Tanov-Emerson Family Favorites

Erica Tanov (antiques and clothing)
1827 – 4th Street
Berkeley, CA 94710
(510) 849-3331

Melissa Gomes (art)
Berkeley, CA
(510) 549-2371

Michael McEwen (lighting)
1420 – 62nd Street
Emeryville, CA 94608
(510) 547-7791

Lydia Ricci (art)
1779 Haight Street
San Francisco, CA 94117
(415) 387-5322

Wanlass Family Favorites

Alameda Antiques By the Bay
(flea market)
Alameda Point Naval Air Station
or send mail to:
PO Box 2230
Alameda, CA 94501
(510) 869-5428
(510) 522-7500

Kindred Spirits (antiques collective)
632 First Street
Benicia, CA 94519
(707) 745-6533

Prize (antiques/vintage finds)
1415 Green Street
San Francisco, CA 94109
(415) 771-7215

Satori Living
(home accents/furniture)
32633 North Scottsdale Road
Building 1
Scottsdale, AZ 85255
(480) 595-6560

Contact us

WITH YOU LIKE TO SEE your home, or a home that you know, celebrated? Is your house full of real family rooms and practical solutions for everyday living? Well, here's your chance. Take some pictures and send them to us—we'd love to see them. It's possible that the next time you're perusing the grocery store magazine or book racks, the glossy cover shot with the fabulous room will be yours. Send us your pictures (or copies, as they will not be returned) to the following address:

Tirzah Wanlass and Jonathan Ortiz
1827 Illinois Street
Vallejo, CA 94590
(707) 648-8878